THE ART
of
Fabric Collage

THE ART

of

Fabric Collage

An Easy
Introduction
to Creative
Sewing

ROSEMARY EICHORN

The Taunton Press

Cover photos: Jack Deutsch

Publisher: Jim Childs
Acquisitions Editor: Jolynn Gower
Assistant Editor: Sarah Coe
Copy Editor: Diane Sinitsky
Art Director: Paula Schlosser
Designer and Layout Artist: Susan Fazekas
Cover Designer: Carol Singer
Photographers: Jack Deutsch, Grey Crawford
Illustrator: Christine Erickson
Indexer: Lynda Stannard

 The Taunton Press
Inspiration for hands-on living™

Printed in the United States of America
10 9 8 7 6 5 4 3 2 1

The Art of Fabric Collage was originally published
in hardcover in 2000 by The Taunton Press, Inc.

The Taunton Press, Inc., 63 South Main Street,
PO Box 5506, Newtown, CT 06470-5506
e-mail: tp@taunton.com

Distributed by Publishers Group West

Library of Congress Cataloging-in-Publication Data
Eichorn, Rosemary.
  The art of fabric collage : an easy introduction to creative sewing /
Rosemary Eichorn.
    p. cm.
  ISBN 1-56158-306-5 hardcover
  ISBN 1-56158-585-8 paperback
  1. Collage. 2. Fabric pictures. 3. Textile crafts. I. Title.
II. Title : Fabric collage.
TT910.E33 2000
746.46—dc21   99—42698
           CIP

To the memory of my mother,
Rosemary Koeberle Doty, whose
love and patience continue to
nurture my creativity and
flow through my bones.

Acknowledgments

I've been blessed by a life filled with people who seem to know what's best for me before that knowledge comes into my awareness. Before I gave serious consideration to writing this book, Lorraine Sintetos presented me with the gift of an outline that she based on her experience in my fabric-collage classes. I'm eternally grateful for her vision and her confidence in the material I had to offer. Lorraine's editorial skills, her writing tutorials, and most of all her friendship are immeasurable gifts without which this book could not have been born. It's been a joyful discovery to learn that crafting with words is much like collaging with fabric.

I've been honored to work with the editorial staff at The Taunton Press. Acquisitions Editor Jolynn Gower gifted me during the early stages of the writing process with her calm confidence in the project and her reassurance that artists can become writers. I'm indebted to Assistant Editor Sarah Coe for her keen observation and intelligent organizing skills. Sarah, photographer Grey Crawford, and his assistant Fernando de Aratanha made the process photo shoot an event of creative collaboration and immense fun.

Without the considerable skills of book designer Susan Fazekas, beauty shot photographer Jack Deutsch, illustrator Christine Erickson, and copy editor Diane Sinitsky, this book would have been as interesting as a three-hour lecture in a darkened room. I'm so appreciative of their talents.

Thanks to Gail Nichols for helping me wake up early enough for water aerobics and our walks up the hill. Without her I would have forgotten to keep moving!

To my daughter Kristen and son Theo, thanks for helping me see what I was going to be when I grew up. To my granddaughter Cherie, thanks for reminding me to continue playing. And to my dear husband Ron, thanks for encouraging me to be all that I can be and loving me through it all.

Before this stellar cast came the students who were my teachers and who asked for the book. To all of you, and especially to those who asked the difficult questions, my deepest appreciation.

Contents

(Photo by Jack Deutsch.)

Introduction

This book is about using a sewing machine as an art tool. It took me much of my lifetime to discover that my sewing machine wasn't just for practical purposes like making clothes and making home furnishings. Even when I got my bachelor's degrees in art and in textiles and clothing, my perception was that I had two different majors and that I'd need to decide which major I'd focus on when I got a job. It took me several more decades to marry my passions—art and textiles.

I hope this book will make the process shorter for you. I'll be introducing you to talents and creativity that you already have, whether you know it or not. You'll learn easy techniques for design and sewing that will enhance any experience you already have. And if you're a real beginner, lucky you. You won't have to overcome some of the hang-ups that some longtime sewers have trouble giving up when they become more creative.

All of my life I wanted to make art, but instead of risking failures—or perhaps success—I kept busy on the periphery of life as an artist. "Life, as it is called, is for most of

us one long postponement," Henry Miller tells us. During the years when my husband Ron and I were raising our family, I had a home business making window coverings for interior designers. All of my friends said, "How creative," but I knew I'd fooled them. I was living in artistic postponement.

Then a healthy mid-life crisis moved me off the dime I'd so comfortably perched on. I was busy making balloon shades for the umpteenth year, and if you sew you probably understand when I say I had lots of meditation time at my sewing machine. I became aware that there was a little creative flame struggling along in my soul, trying desperately to get my attention. When I finally realized that making one more balloon shade was going to bring me to my knees, a group of five women asked me to teach a sewing class.

I accepted the invitation, and I knew that I had no choice but to address the creativity issue. I'd once heard the potter Paulus Barenson say that good teachers teach what they most need to learn themselves. I had no idea how I was going to "teach creativity," but I knew that I had a life to live as an artist and a teacher and that it was time I said yes to it. I only hoped that muses really did exist.

Elizabeth Kubler Ross says there is no such thing as a coincidence, and I believe her. Several textile artists came into my life exactly when I needed them most. Their influence on my artistic development was timely, and each of them helped me fan that smoldering creative flame. One of them was Rachel Clark, whose home is a stone's throw from mine. I'd sat behind Rachel at a church conference in the mid-1970s. I don't remember the conference speaker or her message, but Rachel's outrageous blazer, pieced and quilted in unforgettable colors, radiated a message to my soul. I remember thinking that someday I was going to sew like that.

Years later, I finally met Rachel at a local art show. She had a career as a budding fiber artist and invited me to join her weekly quilting class. I searched to find five fabrics I could piece together, which was the most I'd ever needed to coordinate to decorate a home. Rachel took one look at my pitiful collection and just shook her head. She told me she'd never be satisfied with so few fabrics to work with. I took a flying leap toward my destiny, drove straight to the nearest fabric store to buy quarter-yards of a dozen more fabrics, and I haven't missed a fabric store since.

Soon after, I met Bird Ross through a *Threads* magazine article (issue #40). Bird's instructions for making whole-cloth quilted garments gave me permission to stitch backward as much as to stitch forward. Instead of layering whole pieces of cloth to quilt like Bird did, I layered smaller pieces of fabric side-by-side on a muslin base.

Then I tried her forward and reverse stitching method with free-motion stitching. I had no idea what I was doing, other than realizing that I was having fun feeling my way along, hanging on to my newly found muse by an eyelash.

When I finally took my frayed and raggedy vest experiment from the dryer, I knew I'd discovered something. Handling my vest-in-progress reminded me of a quilt that my Grandma Lil had made for me when I was five years old. That quilt's like the skin horse, well-loved and more than a little threadbare but so comforting to live with. Bird's unique method of finishing garments' edges with squares of fabric also gave me permission to rethink traditional hems and facings. The edging that I now frequently use has vestiges of Bird's influence.

At exactly that same time, I took a class from Therese May at my local junior college. I needed Therese's influence to make something on the sewing machine and to leave threads hanging from it—to discover that the old rules weren't sacred.

Playing with fabric in Therese's class, making masks and hats and silly things I'd never made before, helped me realize how much I loved to sew and that sewing could reach beyond practical ends, that sewing could in fact be art. Therese also helped me realize that I had to take artists off of pedestals, where I'd planted them, so that I could be an artist, too.

I love to garden almost as much as I love to sew. I love gardening's surprises, like the plants that the birds bring that present beautiful bouquets in unexpected places. Or the way a certain plant catches the dew on every little serration of its leaves so that they look like they've been beaded by the garden nymphs.

My perceptions and my collages have changed as I've gardened. I used to think that plants with yellow-green leaves looked like they were lacking nutrients. Now I've discovered how that color of yellow-green is an accent color in a verdant sea. I think I first saw it happen in a collage. Or maybe I put it into a collage after I saw it happen in the garden. I can no longer tell in which direction the information flows. As my garden matures, it looks more and more like a collage. Now there are lots of things—plants and circumstances as well—that I accept and that add color to my life.

The techniques that I explain in this book are stepping stones from here, where we begin together, to there. There can be anywhere you want it to be. There might be gaining the confidence in your ability so that you can design a wall hanging in another favorite technique. There might be scrutinizing the examples in this book and copying them to the best of your ability. Incidentally, you have my permission to do that without guilt. One of the most memorable art exhibits I've ever seen was an exhibit of Picasso's sketch books that he had filled in the years before anyone had heard of Picasso. He copied the masters' work in his sketch books. Of course, they were remarkably good sketches, but he learned his craft by copying the basics, then he found his way to there, where he created art in his particular style. You can, too.

There might be a place of great joy in exploring the creative potential of your sewing machine. My friend Lorraine can make her sewing machine portray ideas and details that I can't even imagine. She says she learned to be a relaxed sewer when she learned to make fabric collages. Having fun without worrying about the outcome has turned her into a skillful sewer.

"Saturday Night Special" by Lorraine Sintetos. My friend Lorraine gained confidence in her creative abilities and increased her sewing skills when she learned fabric-collage techniques. *(Photo by Jack Deutsch.)*

When you want to use your sewing machine to make art, it's important to have a place to start that helps you gain confidence. That's what books and classes are all about. If you'll jump in and use this book to guide you through making a collage, you'll get practice in using your sewing machine as an art tool in a way that's safe and supportive and encouraging. That's what hundreds of my students say they've gotten from my classes, so I'm hoping that by writing this book, I can reach other sewers who want to make art, too.

1
Designing the Collage

Most people who sew clothing or quilts are accustomed to relying on patterns for their projects. Many quilting-technique books give you traditional or original designs to copy, so your creativity is expressed primarily by choosing and combining the colors and prints of your fabrics. The same can be said for sewing clothing from commercial patterns. Because you are given the lines to cut on, your independent decisions are often limited to your choice of a collar style and fabric.

That isn't to say that you can't do a lot to express your individuality and exhibit considerable skill within these limitations, however, working from a pattern is reassuring because you know what the finished project is supposed to look like. You have instructions to help you create a quilt or a garment very much like the one in the picture. So for some people used to working from patterns, the thought of working without

one is intimidating. They feel they are expected to dive from the high board when they aren't even sure they know how to dog paddle.

If you've never created designs independently, this collage experience can forever change the way you create with fabric. You'll discover you have unlimited flexibility in choosing motifs because with fabric collage you won't be restricted to using only simple-shaped pieces of fabric that are large enough to have their edges turned under, as in traditional appliqué techniques.

After exploring fiber collage in one of my workshops, Mary Anhaltzer, an emerging artist in the art quilt world, realized she had unlimited freedom in choosing design elements. Embracing that freedom was an important key in helping her unleash her artistic capabilities. No design has an edge too tightly curved, too pointy, or too complex to use. Just think of the gamut of sub-

"Dream City" (28 in. by 22 in.): A surreal dream suggested the watery cityscape theme for this wall hanging. *(Photo by Jack Deutsch.)*

ject matter printed on textiles that are available to you!

Sometimes just thinking about starting a new project using an unfamiliar technique can open the doors to self-doubt. My dad, a self-reliant Midwesterner, once said, "I always figured that if someone else can do it, I can do it, too." Those are the words that I have tried to remember when I see something beautiful that looks too complex to do myself. I've come to tack on my own ending, "…if my desire is strong enough."

Armed with your resolve and a desire to create a wonderful collage without a pattern to copy, you'll find it easier than you ever thought to take on this design project if you do it one step at a time. I'll help you

get started by giving you guidelines for fabric selection and by discussing design techniques that will make it easier to visualize a collage layout.

As you work on this collage, think of it as a process, rather than as a project. This is not a project in which you will know how the work will end before it begins. We never know everything about a day when we enter it, but we enter it anyway. During the process, you'll discover that you have your own notions about making the next one. Remember that you are not being tested on your artistic abilities or sewing skills, although as you create your collage, you'll be making strides toward becoming better at both.

But I Don't Know How to Sew!

Before you get started, let's talk about your sewing experience, or lack of it. Many experienced quilters confess that they don't really know how to sew; they just use the machine for joining two pieces of fabric together, one short seam after another. Those who think of yourselves as "sewing challenged" will be surprised at how your sewing skills will improve as you proceed through this project.

On each collage there is a lot of stitching that I consider renegade sewing—playing with your sewing machine to see what you can coax from it that will help you make an artistic statement. As you'll see, renegade sewing also means breaking some rules that someone probably told you never to break. This is very different from grown-up sewing. That's my term for the sewing we learned as youngsters in 4-H Clubs and home economics classes or from professional sewing instructors. Grown-up sewing is tailoring jackets, constructing couturier-quality garments, assembling sophisticated traditional quilts, and fabricating precisely-measured soft furnishings for home decoration. Grown-up sewing is a great joy to many of us and an anathema to others. I believe that one is not better or worse than the other, just very different.

Believe me, I know the thrill of accomplishment that comes when I've successfully sewn together 12 converging points and ironed them flat. On the other hand, renegade sewing gives a different kind of thrill—it incorporates serendipity and play. Renegade sewing is so surprisingly freeing and fun that even some of the most determined perfectionists among my students have gone home with their adrenaline

pumping from the excitement of learning to play at their sewing machines.

If you've always wanted to sew those 12 perfect seams but were sure that your skills would leave you disappointed, now as a renegade sewer you can give it a try. If you

Skillful sewing techniques take a back seat to playful exploration of a sewing machine's potential when doing fabric collage. (Photo by Jack Deutsch.)

"Azitlan Couple" (43 in. by 32 in.): When Mary Anhaltzer incorporated raw edges into her art quilts, she found new freedom in creating her beautiful collages. (Photo by Mary Anhaltzer.)

Using a Template for Design Inspiration

Here's a design activity using a template that my students enjoy. This is an old art school exercise that will help you visualize an interesting organization of shapes on your collage and will provide you with a guide for your design. Photocopy the template shown below on stiff paper, or trace it onto a piece of template plastic or a recycled file folder. Cut off the text, then cut along the indicated lines. The opening of this template measures 3 in. by 4 in. Multiply 3 and 4 by any other number to arrive at a larger size for your collage. For example, multiply 3 by 6 (18) and 4 by 6 (24). Your 18-in. by 24-in. finished collage will be the same proportion as this template.

To use the template, place it over color photographs from magazines, calendars, or coffee-table art books. Turning the photos upside down will help you get away from seeing particular subject matter. You're looking for designs instead of subject matter to frame. Slowly slide the template around to get different views and observe the images in the window diagonally as well as vertically and horizontally. Look for a pleasing arrangement of shapes and colors within the template. Ask yourself the following questions:

- What color combinations strike you?
- What shapes or lines of movement catch your attention?
- Does the composition become more or less interesting when you move the template?
- Is there a pattern of light and dark that keeps your eye moving through the composition?

When you've isolated a composition that pleases you, it can be used as a design "blueprint" for a collage. Use a bit of removable tape to hold your template in position so you can refer to it when you start laying out your design. You can also place a piece of tracing paper over the composition and trace the major elements of the design, using written notes to yourself and perhaps using colored pencils to indicate how you'd like to use this design. Is your composition beginning to suggest some fabrics from your stash that will work as a starting point?

A template will help you isolate design ideas from magazines, photographs, and nature. The opening of this template measures 3 in. x 4 in. To arrive at a larger size for your collage that will have the same proportion as this template, multiply 3 and 4 by any other number. For example, multiply 3 by 6 (18) and 4 by 6 (24) to come up with a collage that will measure 18 in. x 24 in.

Moving a template across a photograph in a magazine isolates an image that can be used to inspire a collage layout. *(Photo by Grey Crawford.)*

succeed, great! If your results fall short of perfection, you can add your sample to a collage and hide the less successful areas under another fabric or a trim. By the time you've stitched over the whole piece and laundered it to a lovely texture, you'll have created a collage you'll be proud of.

Be assured that your natural creativity will flourish as you learn the innovative design and sewing techniques of fabric collage. There will be lots of opportunity to use your sewing machine, and by the end of this project, your free-motion sewing skills will have improved immensely. You'll even be better prepared to do first-class traditional machine-quilting, if that's your inclination. In the process of learning, there are no mistakes—and anything you do will end up looking just great. As you'll see, there are a number of easy ways to refine your fabric designs as you go, just as a painter adds layers of color to develop her designs. One of my students expressed the spirit of fiber collage when she quipped, "There aren't any mistakes in fiber collage—just design opportunities!"

Finding Inspiration

A collage begins with an idea. You may want it to reflect your interests—growing orchids, exploring tide pools, or baking cakes. You might be inspired by a particular piece of fabric that says jungles or Japan or hog heaven. Sometimes a Big Life Event, such as a family reunion or the loss of a pet, will give impulse to the artwork. Or perhaps the idea that motivates you will be your challenge to yourself to work with a part of the color spectrum that's unfamiliar to you. A scrap of vintage fabric from a tag sale, a remnant of your grandmother's apron, or a reproduction historic fabric might also

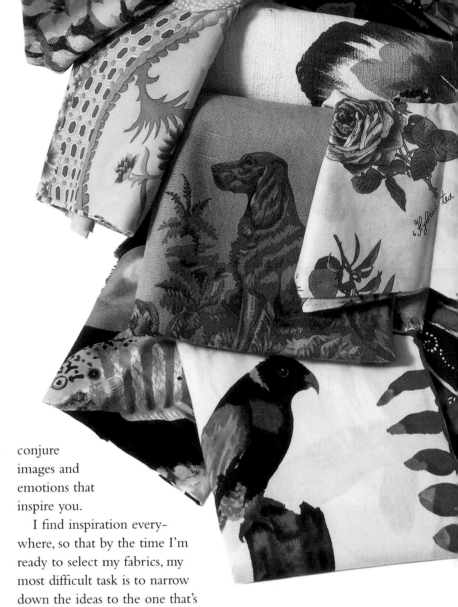

conjure images and emotions that inspire you.

I find inspiration everywhere, so that by the time I'm ready to select my fabrics, my most difficult task is to narrow down the ideas to the one that's most compelling. Incorporating too many ideas and too many different techniques into one project can be distracting, so I try to keep my focus on one good concept and use only enough variety in techniques to enhance the concept.

Inspiration lies in wait for you, too. Think "collage" when you look at decorating magazines and travel ads. Check out the greeting cards the next time you're in a stationery store. If there's one that you're especially drawn to for any reason, bring it home and put it where you will see it often. What can it teach you about the qualities of color you

Textiles with specific themes are plentiful and often provide the inspiration for a collage.
(Photo by Grey Crawford.)

Details found in nature, such as the lichen on this rock, can suggest stitching texture patterns that can be used on a collage. *(Photo by Rosemary Eichorn.)*

Translating Inspiration into Designs

For your first small collage project, you'll need about 20 different quarter-yards (or smaller amounts) of fabric. I use as many as 15 to 20 fabrics in each collage, but I begin by pulling even more possibilities than that from my stash. Here are some guidelines to consider as you make your selections.

Begin by choosing two or three fabrics with large motifs: flowers, fruit, festoons, animals, or images in novelty prints. I often begin with a fabric designed for home decoration or a vintage fabric with large motifs, such as those used for slipcovers and draperies. Your motif fabrics should contain a number of different hues and should have some colors in common. These motif prints will establish the theme and dominant color scheme of your collage and will provide the focal points in your composition.

Next, choose 15 or more background prints that pick up colors from the large motifs. Be sure to choose several fabrics in bright colors that you'll use sparingly. Include some small geometrics, dots, plaids, and stripes to add variety. For your first project, leave your solid-colored fabrics in their storage place.

For more about design principles, read pp. 21-25 before you begin to design your collage. You can refer to those principles as you go, if you feel you need a compass to keep you on the right track.

love? Which subjects elicit a response from you? Are you attracted to realistic designs or are abstract designs more appealing to you? Lately, I've been looking at historic textiles and I'm seeing so many possibilities, such as color schemes that are new to me and motifs that provide inspiration for surface design.

Look for textures as you walk outdoors, and if possible, photograph them for future reference. Paint peeling from buildings, fungus on tree bark, oil floating in puddles, and miniscule beads of dew clustered on spider webs are a few of the texture inspirations I've seen recently. My own garden frequently inspires my palette. For example, I've noticed that artemisia, a plant with cool gray-green foliage, enhances the bright pink and deep magenta of the geranium growing through it. Pure green foliage seems even brighter next to artemisia's gray tones. New buds among fading flowers seem even more fresh and tender because of the contrast. Many of my collages reflect discoveries like these.

Fabrics with large motifs provide inspiration for a collage's theme and help establish its color scheme. *(Photo by Grey Crawford.)*

Here are some guidelines to help you choose background fabrics that will enhance your motif prints.

• *Vary the values (relative lightness or darkness) of the colors.* If your fabrics are all close in value, your collage will lack the contrast necessary to make it exciting. It will seem to be made of a single piece of yardage, printed with a "cheater" quilt design. To start, push the values you select to their extremes. For example, purple can range from the deepest black-purple like the color of eggplant, often called aubergine, to a pale, transparent amethyst. Look for prints that contain both the darkest and lightest shades of the colors you're using. Going from very dark to very light values will make your collage sparkle and provide drama. If you want more subdued results, choose fabrics with closer values.

• *Vary the scale of the patterns, including large, medium, and small prints.* Contrasting small patterns to large ones will help make your collage more interesting. Keep in mind that when you use a small-scale print, you'll get an effect from its colors, but its design will simply look like a texture in a collage. For example, suppose you've used a print with tiny daisies to fit in with your flower garden theme. By the time your textured vest comes out of the dryer, no one will be able to distinguish those daisies from scrambled eggs. Therefore, don't be afraid to select any small- or medium-sized print for its color, regardless of its theme.

Use unexpected colors to enliven a bland combination.

• *Use unexpected colors to enliven a bland combination.* It's tempting to buy stunning coordinated fabric groups, assured that they'll harmonize. But too much harmony is often boring. Years ago I was making a Christmas quilt in crisp reds and greens when it struck me that the little patches were too perfectly matched in hue. I looked for the least Christmasy green I could find, which turned out to be almost khaki colored, then I added several spots of it. This ugly duckling became a beauty as it created surprise and interest. My color composition became dynamic instead of bland. Some of my favorite collages contain a number of color combinations that I loved as a child but was criticized for using. Among them are khaki green and aqua, and magenta and teal. Be fearless about using colors that supposedly don't "go together." If you like them, use them. They will express your unique color sense.

• *When choosing fabrics, look at them in the proportion in which they'll be used.* Suppose that your motif fabric contains deep blue and orange, and you've found two very bright prints in these colors that you might use as accents. If you lay these three lengths side-by-side, you might reject the blue fabric as too intense and the orange fabric as gaudy. Try tucking the blue fabric under the motif fabric so that just a ½-in. slice of it shows, then do the same for the orange. When you see the potential accent fabrics in these smaller proportions, you have a better idea of how these fabrics might work in a collage.

It may take some resourcefulness to create a work surface that won't be needed for something else and won't give you a backache. You might recycle a 3-ft. by 6-ft. drafting table or an inexpensive blank door. A rotary cutting mat can be placed on top of either one. I use a 3-ft. by 6-ft. cutting mat and do my designing right on top of it. Ideally (ergonomically speaking), your worktable should be at a height where you can stand with your spine erect and your elbows bent at 90 degrees when your hands rest on the front edge of the table. This is often 10 in. higher than the average work surface. There's plenty of room underneath a worktable at this height for storage drawers.

Gently slanting your work surface to bring your work closer to you will put minimum stress on your lower back. A phone book or block of wood can be used to raise the back of the worktable 3 in. to 4 in. I keep a 9-in. step stool by my worktable so I can step on it to reach the far edge of the table. I can also rest one foot on the step stool while I'm working, which also takes stress off the lower back.

Adding a margin to motifs when they're cut out will allow for fraying in the final stages of the collage process. *(Photo by Grey Crawford.)*

Creating a Sample Collage

Let's try a sample project. For a sample project measuring approximately 18 in. by 24 in., you'll need the following materials:

- ½ yd. muslin for underlining
- Sharp, 4-in. or 5-in. sewing or craft scissors
- A rotary cutter and a small mat
- Glass-headed pins
- A work surface on which you can leave your project undisturbed
- Your fabrics
- Your trims

Begin by cutting a rectangular muslin underlining 18 in. by 24 in. and spreading it on a flat surface. It should be in a place where you can leave it undisturbed until you have finished laying out your design.

Lay out your fabrics near your design area, then choose several of the theme fabrics with large motifs. For your sample collage, I look for designs that are at least the size of my fist. Use short-bladed scissors to cut out the motif pieces, leaving a border ⅛ in. to 3/16 in. wide around each piece. Loosely woven fabrics, such as cotton drapery fabrics, require the larger allowance. Cut out more motifs than you think you'll need so you will have plenty of options as you compose your collage.

CUTTING OUT MOTIFS

Look beyond the obvious when you're cutting out whole motifs. I made my first collaged vest out of scraps left over from other projects. To my disappointment, I couldn't find a single intact tiger on one of my favorite prints. But I cut out their fore parts and hind parts anyway, and the tigers seemed to tell me what to do with them. They begged to peek out from behind big flowers and to flaunt their tails in unexpected places. In the end, that vest was more interesting than it would have been if I'd appliquéd whole tigers onto the surface of my collage (see the photo on the facing page). Now I look for interesting ways to cut apart motifs so they can surprise and delight the eye.

When I cut out motifs, I also become better acquainted with the colors I'll be using. I look carefully at my fabric for colors that I might have missed at first glance—the "hidden colors." Some sewers have identified their palettes for flattering clothing colors, and as a result they ignore whole sections of the color spectrum in their artwork simply because they don't wear those colors. For example, someone who wears warm, earthy colors might fail to notice the icy-blue highlights on an autumn leaf print. Yet such hidden colors are often just what give life to a color scheme. You may realize that an odd color you'd never choose for a sweater is exactly what you need to make your collage sing.

I've also noticed that when a color is not in current fashion, it is likely to become a hidden color. Remember the years when you couldn't find a good variety of yellow fabrics? During that time it became a cliché to add a bit of yellow to save a quilt's color scheme from appearing too trite.

Later, you'll outline these motifs with machine stitch-es, leaving their borders to fray in the laundering process. With experience, you'll learn the fraying characteristics of various fabrics and use them accordingly. For example, many vintage drapery fab-rics and contemporary home-decorating fabrics launder to a soft, velvety edge. When I cut out these motifs, I leave a slightly wider margin to fray. On the other hand, some of the finely woven cotton batik fabrics barely fray at all, so I leave a scant ⅛ in. beyond the motifs cut from these fabrics. That's enough for the stitching to hold without pulling out in handling and laundering.

LAYING OUT MOTIFS

To begin your layout, arrange three of your most eye-catching motif pieces on the muslin. These are the focal points around which your design will develop. Have one of them more prominent than the other two. This can be accomplished by having

The author's first collaged vest sports tigers peeking from behind fabrics textured with machine stitching. Layering motifs behind other fabrics gives the impression of a third dimension. (*Photo by Jack Deutsch.*)

By the Way

If there is one unbreakable rule for making a collage it's play. Have fun with the colors, shapes, and textures, and forget that you're designing. Later on you'll have many opportunities to assess the overall design, so for now put a gag on the voice that says, "This will never work" or "Am I doing this right?" Answer any questions that begin "Should I worry if..." with a resounding "No!" And unless your family and friends have proved supportive through some unusual projects, it's best to ban them from your work area. You can make exceptions for children under seven, who seem to intuitively understand and support your collage-making. Give them a pair of scissors.

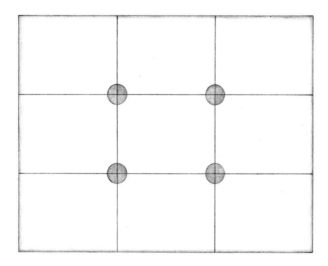

When you divide your design into thirds vertically and horizontally, any of the intersections are good for positioning the focal points.

dynamic composition than a "bull's-eye" placement.

Play with the arrangement of these motif pieces until they're in a composition that seems attractive to you. If you did the template activity at the beginning of this chapter, use it as a guide for placing your cut-out motifs. As I work, I've learned to resist the temptation to pin pieces in place until I've composed the entire design, including the background. Once I start pinning, the pieces seem unalterably fixed, and I stop considering my options.

FILLING IN THE BACKGROUND

Now you're ready to cut out some interesting shapes to use to fill in around your motifs. Use a range of fabrics in light, medium, and dark values. Vary the size of the pieces you cut as well as their shapes. When a fabric has a motif or curved or jagged design lines, it is easier to cut interesting, irregular shapes from it by following an imaginary edge of the printed design. A plain fabric or one with a small all-over design can be a challenge to cut into an interesting shape.

If you and your scissors can't seem to cut anything but rectangles from your rectangles of fabric, then liberate yourself by using a rotary cutter. Lay your fabric flat on a cutting mat. Then, reminding yourself that cut-

one larger than the others, or in a brighter color, or with more value contrast within its design.

Here's an easy trick to help you place your center of interest. If you visually divide your design area into thirds, both vertically and horizontally, each of the points at which these imaginary lines intersect makes a visually pleasing place for your center of interest. Using one of these areas for placement of your focal point will create a more

By the Way

Do you have trouble cutting intricate shapes out of limp fabric? If so, give each side of the fabric a good spritz of heavy-duty spray starch and press dry. Now your fabric will behave like paper.

Arranging theme motifs on a muslin underlining is the first step in designing a collage. (Photo by Grey Crawford.)

One of the most exciting discoveries I've made as a teacher is that collages that come back on the second day of a workshop are nothing like those that were started on the first day. I've heard students say, "My collage took on a life of its own" or "I felt out of control and had no idea where this design was taking me." If this happens to you, surrender! Your creation will have more heart than one with an imposed plan.

Sometimes you see a story unfolding as you cut out motifs or assemble them on your collage. It's like being a child moving toys around in a sandbox. Long forgotten memories arise, and the collage becomes subtly autobiographical. Or you see a new relationship between motifs, which suggests another kind of story. Let your mind wander and take you with it. It's sometimes difficult at first for very organized people to give up control and let their imaginations take over, but it's a perfectly safe way to let yourself go.

Perhaps hearing about one of my experiences will help you understand what I mean by letting your collage have its way. I was once cutting roses from a vintage drapery fabric and

> ### "My collage took on a life of its own."

arranging them as the focal point on a vest. What I had in mind was using a rose garden theme—pretty but uninspired. The deep magenta of the roses was set off by a background of clear aqua. I opened my drawer of teal fabrics, and a favorite ocean wave fabric seemed to jump into my hands. Well, it certainly didn't fit in with my rose garden theme, but I wanted to see that color included. Before I had a chance to censor myself, I cut out powerful, swirling wave shapes and began arranging them among my roses.

My insistence on using the teal fabric seemed strange to me. Then I became aware of a throbbing pain in my hand, where a large rose thorn had attacked as I was pruning a rosebush earlier that day. I noticed the nature of that pain; it ebbed and flowed like the ocean waves in the teal print. As I continued composing my vest, I thought about some things in my life that had come in waves: small swells of challenge that were followed by billows of joy, fallow times followed by bursts of intense creativity. I titled the vest, "It Always Comes in Waves." The vest had more meaning for me and was much more intriguing than the garden vest I had planned.

ting lines can be straight or curved or combinations of both, use a twisting wrist motion as you roll your cutter back and forth. Voilà—a random shape! Each cut into the fabric will leave an irregular edge behind. Use that edge as one side of the next shape you cut.

Don't worry about cutting shapes to fit a particular spot on your collage: You aren't cutting them to fit together like puzzle pieces. Cut good-sized pieces, about the size of your palm or larger, because small ones can be frustrating. They shift and migrate, exposing the muslin underlining, whereas larger pieces are easier to control.

Using a small rotary cutter aids in cutting out interesting random shapes for background fabrics. *(Photo by Grey Crawford.)*

Variety in texture, color, and motif is unified by overall stitching. *(Photo by Jack Deutsch.)*

Irregular outer edges of motifs create beautiful shapes in the negative spaces between them. Play up these shapes to create interesting layouts by placing fabrics that contrast in color, value, and texture behind the motifs. *(Photo by Grey Crawford.)*

When you place the fabric pieces in your collage, it's important that the upper fabric overlaps the lower by at least ½ in. If your overlap is too skimpy, your fabrics are likely to slip apart while you're sewing them down, allowing the muslin underlining to show. Don't worry if you end up with five or six layers of fabric in one place and only two in another. The collage will look just fine after the pieces have been stitched down and laundered.

For the background, choose a fabric that you think might be attractive alongside a major motif. Slip it in place under an edge of the motif, then consider the following:

- Does it enhance the motif fabric?

- Are you creating interesting shapes?

- Is it hard to tell where one fabric begins and the other ends? If so, is the blended effect enhancing your design or detracting from it?

Refer to the design principles on pp. 21-25 if you're having trouble trusting your intuition on which fabric to place where. Keep adding fabric shapes until your design is developing to your satisfaction—and remember that you will be able to return to an area later to fine-tune the composition. Because you'll want to be able to make changes easily, don't pin anything down as you lay out your designs.

Look for interesting shapes that are formed in the space around motifs. These shapes are known as negative shapes, or ground. Your motif is referred to as a positive shape, or figure. The irregular edge of your motif creates shapes on the background of the collage that can help make an interesting design. For instance, a light-colored background fabric placed near a dark-colored motif with an intriguing edge causes a second interesting shape to appear from the light-colored fabric.

Think of the edges of your collage as the edges of a continent silhouetted against the

background fabric. The background fabric is metaphorically the ocean surrounding your collage continent. If you create your collage continent with deep bays and ragged peninsulas, it's far more interesting than it would be with a shallow, predictable saw-toothed coastline.

To get this effect, place the motifs and cut-out shapes with the most intriguing outlines at the edges of your designs. Then create beautiful negative shapes by having some small, some medium, and some large areas protruding into the open areas of the background fabric.

Islands of varying sizes adrift on the background will add further interest. Create them as you'd see them on a map. The larger islands are closest to the shores of the continents, and the islands get progressively smaller as you move farther out into the oceans. Our minds like this order because it fits the natural order of the universe.

Conversely, if you wish to establish more tension in your compositions, experiment with rearranging the natural order. Paying attention to these negative shapes can help you create more compelling artwork.

As you continue to design, pause at intervals to assess your collage. An easy way to get a fresh perspective on your work is to step back from it 6 ft. to 8 ft. You'll need a greater distance when you design collages on a larger format. Some people like to use a reducing glass, which acts like a telescope turned backwards. It helps you see your work as though you're viewing it from a distance. If you wear glasses, take them off. My best tool is to squint so that the details blur and I see only patterns of dark and light and shapes of color.

Looking at your work, ask yourself if you're bothered by anything that doesn't seem quite right. For some criteria to help you assess your collage, read through the section on design principles on pp. 21–25, then come back for a second look. It's not too late to make changes. At this point, I'll sometimes eliminate all of the pieces cut from one or two of my original fabric choices because the colors or the patterns just aren't working with the design that is emerging.

ADDING TRIMS AND RIBBONS

If you plan to use trims or ribbons, add them as you develop your design. This will integrate them into the overall arrangement rather than giving the appearance that they are floating on top of the collage as an afterthought. You can use the trims in many ways: to add sparkle and emphasis, to create movement, or to help unify the composition. Consider using novelty patches, lace medallions, or ribbons with printed messages to add character and to amplify your theme.

When you apply a narrow trim, such as soutache braid or a slender ribbon, experiment with it. Try knotting it every inch or so to create texture, or make loops to circle your motifs. You could also let the trim meander across your collage, sometimes disappearing under a fabric edge and reappearing several inches away. Incidentally, that now-you-see-it-now-you-don't application

Cutting up 12 in. of a special braid into three pieces makes it possible to stretch the braid out so that it appears as if a much longer piece was used. *(Photo by Grey Crawford.)*

In addition to fabric stores, look for sheer polyester and nylon ribbons in stores that sell gift wraps and in florist's shops. (Photo by Jack Deutsch.)

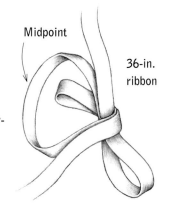

TYING A BOW

1. Make two rabbit ear loops.

2. Tie an overhand knot with the two ears.

Midpoint

36-in. ribbon

is a thrifty way to make the most of expensive trims. By cutting a half-yard of costly ribbon into several shorter lengths and tucking the cut ends under the edges of fabric shapes, you can create the illusion that a longer piece of extravagant trim is weaving through your collage.

When you use wide ribbons and laces, don't simply stitch them down in a straight line. Loop them, pleat them, or tie them in large knots that are loose enough to be stitched down flat. Fabrics with interesting lengthwise stripes can be cut into bands that can be treated like ribbons. You can make a simple bow that can easily be stitched flat if you follow the steps shown in the illustration above. This big bow is stunning when made from a sheer polyester gift-wrap rib-

bon. These ribbons are durable, launder beautifully, and add a touch of elegance to fiber collage.

PINNING THE PIECES TOGETHER

When you're satisfied that all your fabric pieces and trims are where you want them, pin them down, being generous with your pins. Put one pin in the center of each large motif, then pin down all the points at which neighboring fabrics overlap. I like glass-headed pins because they don't get lost as easily under loose edges of fabric.

Sometimes I use a water-soluble UHU glue stick to hold down a length of ribbon or trim or to control a fine detail such as an insect antenna or a leafy tendril. However, I don't use them to attach all of my fabric

By the Way

Scratches from pinpoints aren't inevitable. I've discovered that I can avoid scratches if I run the point back down through just the top layer of fabric and push the pin all the way in to its head.

Use more pins than you think you'll need to anchor the collage before stitching. (Photo by Grey Crawford.)

pieces to the muslin because in some areas there are so many layers to be attached to each other that each would need to be glued to the one below it. When you're finished pinning, you should be able to pick up your collaged underlining from each side without causing any fabric pieces to come adrift or any fabric edges to flutter.

ATTACHING THE BACKING FABRIC

At this point, you have assembled the top two layers of your three-layer collage and you're ready to attach the backing. I often wait until I've finished my collage to choose my backing fabric. By then I have a better idea of what colors I want to use or how I want the backing to carry out my theme.

For this first project, the simplest backing to use is a single piece of fabric. Choose one that is compatible with your collage in color and theme. Begin by laying the backing fabric wrong side up on your cutting surface and placing the collage on it so that wrong sides are together. Make sure that both layers are perfectly flat, then add a few more pins

to hold the collage in place and cut around it, using the collage as your pattern. You're ready now to conquer free-motion stitching and become a full-fledged renegade sewer. Refer to chapter 3 on free-motion stitching for instructions.

Design Principles: Assessing Your Work

As I've suggested earlier, your collage consists of an idea, or theme, and a layout, or design, of the pieces of fabric that express your idea. Design is where most of us get hung up.

In the visual arts, there are always design problems that need to be solved. But there are also ways of arriving at solutions, used in successful works of art through the ages, known as design principles. As I've introduced fabric collage, I've encouraged you to let go of some "rules" that you inherited when you learned to sew, such as "stitch, then press" and "finish raw edges." Now I'm introducing design principles that may

Unity in design can be created by choosing fabrics that relate to each other in idea. Here it's animal prints, as well as in color—gold, brown, and black. *(Photo by Grey Crawford.)*

sound like rules, but I prefer to call them guidelines.

Each artist has her own list of design principles she finds most useful. These principles act as guides, helping the artist assess her results as she works, usually without conscious thought. Before you can do this, you must be aware of these principles and make them a part of your art process. Then you can let go of them so you are not intellectualizing every design decision you make. Following are some design principles that I consistently use in my work. They'll help you assess your work without having to take time out for a college course in Basic Design Theory (although I recommend it if you're even slightly interested).

UNITY

Unity holds the various design elements together so that the viewer is first struck by an overall image. After getting an impression of the whole, the viewer is drawn in to examine the details.

One way to achieve unity in a collage is to select a theme and have all of the motif fabrics contribute to that theme. The jungle animals in your collage may have come from five different commercial fabrics along with one that you created using rubber stamps,

but you have created unity by consistently using fabrics based on a single idea.

Visual unity results from using fabrics that relate to one another beyond their theme. Let's suppose that when you choose your jungle fabrics, one is printed on a background of black and white zebra stripes, several are in soft summer colors, and the rest are in intense crayon hues. Moreover, your fabrics run the gamut from sophisticated upholstery cottons to prints for children's play clothes. A collage of these fabrics presents visual chaos.

There's a remedy. When you look for your theme fabrics, choose ones with some mutual colors. This doesn't mean that if your motif fabric has a gold tiger with a soft yellow, burgundy, and brown background, you are limited to these four colors. Instead, you might find another jungle print that repeats the gold and brown and then adds a bit of deep blue and a variety of greens. Now you can look for related fabrics repeating the blue and greens. Expanding your palette by adding accent colors from several fabrics gives you far more fabric choices—and will result in an interesting collage.

One trick that I use to alter the palette suggested by a certain fabric is to cut away all or part of the background. For example, I see bunches of deep purple grapes and rosy apples that inspire me, but the bright turquoise background is too intense for the rich color scheme I've envisioned. I'll remove the background so I can use the grape motif with other fabrics that would clash with the turquoise. You'll find that by using parts of a print, you can add fabrics that would otherwise fail to support the palette you're working with.

Another method used to create visual unity is to

Overlapping seemingly unrelated motifs helps to create unity in a design. *(Photo by Jack Deutsch.)*

The hand motif in this collage layout becomes dominant because of the shift in value between the light hand and the dark fabrics behind it. *(Photo by Grey Crawford.)*

repeat shapes. On one collage you might use round plums, round cabbage roses, and the curving loops of a ribbon tied in a bow. The repetition of these curving shapes unifies your design.

An easy way to achieve unity is to place major design elements close together. A long-stemmed flower and a leopard seem unrelated until the stem overlaps the leopard and suddenly they seem to belong together.

Fortunately, texture, which also acts as a unifying element, is built into the construction of fabric collage. Once your collage is covered by free-motion stitching, it will be laundered so it comes out puckered and softly frayed all over. What once appeared to be many sort-of-related scraps of fabric have magically transformed into a unified design.

DOMINANCE

Dominance refers to a point of emphasis in your artwork. Like a painting, your collage needs a focal point to create a strong design. A focal point attracts the viewer's eye and engages her interest. The eye then moves on to other interesting but less obvious elements of your design. The more contrast there is around a motif, the more important the motif will appear. Contrast is achieved by a shift in the color, value, size, shape,

or texture between two adjacent pieces of fabric.

A motif that contrasts in value to the surrounding fabric, such as a dark purple fish against a light blue wave, says, "Look at me!" He is the dominant character in the artwork. The viewer is then drawn through the composition by secondary points of interest—a small octopus, a clump of pale pink coral, and a gray-green fish half the size of the purple one. The secondary points of interest are smaller or contrast less with their backgrounds than the main motif. If you don't make other elements subordinate to the main motif, the viewer will be confused. When four equally engaging motifs demand attention, none of them dominates.

While I'm on the subject of visual impact and numbers, I believe that odd numbers of motifs are more intriguing than equal numbers. Whether I'm adding

The vertical balance in this mandala illustrates symmetric, or formal, balance. The two halves closely mirror each other. *(Photo by Grey Crawford.)*

leaf clusters or bead embellishments, I typically use three or five rather than two or four. Odd numbers tend to captivate the eye and keep it exploring the composition, while even numbers vie for the viewer's attention, eventually boring her.

BALANCE

Balance is expressed in one of two ways: Two halves of a composition can mirror one another (symmetric or formal balance, as shown in the bottom photo on p. 23), or the motifs can shift around like five kids on a teeter-totter until they've found a way to balance it (asymmetric or informal balance, as shown in the photo below). Asymmetric balance is dynamic, while symmetry suggests quiet repose. One is not better than the other—except in terms of the effect that you want to create.

Asymmetric balance is casual and dynamic, creating an impression of movement within the design. *(Photo by Jack Deutsch.)*

For your first collage project, try designing with asymmetric balance. Your challenge is to figure out how to make the two sides balance visually when they're not the same. Think of those kids on the teeter-totter as you try to create balance. Two elements to work with are size and color.

Size Large pieces of fabric seem "weightier" than small ones. Likewise, one large motif will balance a group of smaller motifs.

Color Bright, light, and vivid colors advance, making them appear heavier than dark or dull colors, which recede. So a small piece of bright yellow fabric might seem equal in weight to a large piece of medium blue fabric.

As you work on your collage, if one side seems more eye-catching than the other, try adding lighter-colored or larger pieces to the less exciting side to give it more visual weight. Or subdue bright colors by covering them with a darker shade of tulle or by using a fabric marking pen to tone them down.

PROPORTION

Proportion is the ratio of the size of one design in the artwork to the size of a design on another part of it or to the whole piece. Your designs will be more compelling if you vary both the sizes of the prints on your fabrics and the sizes of the pieces of fabric that you cut.

To help you visualize what I mean, think of your collage as a rocky landscape. Your motifs are represented by the boulders that dominate the scene and are typically cut in larger pieces or clusters of pieces that work together as one. Attractive formations are created by the large rocks resting against those boulders. These rocks are suggested by your medium-sized prints. Your small prints and fine-textured fabrics are the stones and gravel that fill the empty spaces around the rocks.

If you cut a palm-sized piece of a small print, it will appear and disappear under the other pieces of the collage that overlap it, giving the impression that it is many small pieces. These gravelly areas might also be represented in your collage by small amounts of a glitzy novelty fabric or a bit of bright accent color. These will provide sparkle in an otherwise cautious and possibly boring color scheme.

Scale is a close relative of proportion; it is another word for size. Scale can provide an element of surprise in your collage. If you alter the expected scale of, say, a cat and a human, with the cat appearing 10 times larger than the human, you have already made a statement. It could be a statement of the artist's esteem for cats or it might say something about the artist's submission to cats. At any rate, by changing the expected imagery in your artwork, you automatically engage the viewer when she begins to speculate about your motives.

Variety in the proportion of light, medium, and dark colors and large, medium, and small prints avoids monotony. *(Photo by Jack Deutsch.)*

Surprise viewers by changing the expected scale of objects in your collage. *(Photo by Grey Crawford.)*

These design principles are based on the observation and analysis of successful art created over the centuries. If you'd like to understand more about the principles of design, visit museums and galleries and look at books of fine art. For another perspective, become a keen observer of nature. Take your template from p. 10 on your walks, and observe what you see by using the template to create a frame around a variety of scenes and vignettes. Novelist Marcel Proust tells us, "The real voyage of discovery consists not in seeking new landscapes but in having new eyes."

2

Developing a Fabric Stash

Selecting fabric for your collage is where the fun begins and your creativity blossoms. The fabrics you choose will not only provide color but also will help you create texture, contrast, movement, and depth. Your prints and colors will establish the theme and the mood of your collage. Think of your fabric collection as a painter thinks of her palette. Few artists work only with pure color. They blend paints to gray them or change their value; they juxtapose colors for contrast; and they use touches of color to suggest movement and depth. You'll be doing the same with your fabrics.

Assessing Your Stash

If you're a typical sewer or a quilter, you have a stash of 1-yd. to 3-yd. lengths of fabric that you couldn't live without and some that you can't seem to use. You might have acquired them for a project you lost

interest in or simply out of your need to possess them. Take a good look at your fabric collection. It comprises the first choices on your palette. What do they tell you about your relationship to colors and fabrics? Do you choose fabrics predominantly from one narrow band of the spectrum (i.e., "I only work with jewel tones") or do you go for the whole rainbow?

Have you made most of your selections spontaneously with little regard for color or theme, or have you been meticulously collecting fabrics of a particular type, like "museum-reproduction prints of Early American vintage" or "contemporary ethnic"?

Where would you like to go with your color experiments? Broaden your range or narrow it? Expand the way you use the hues you like best or explore new color families?

EXPANDING YOUR PALETTE

You are about to embark on a creative mission. If you were a painter, you'd be seriously handicapped if you had only tubes of red and blue paint to work with, so be honest with yourself as you assess your stash. Does its range of color inspire you? Are you limited to working with a box of 8 crayons, or are you using the big box of 64? You owe it to yourself to have an inventory of fabrics that contains a wide variety of colors, prints, and motifs. These form your palette, which is the range of colors you use. They are also the visual textures you have at your disposal. Most important, your fabrics are the heart and soul of your designs because you have chosen them to convey your message.

"Midsummer Medley": It's helpful to have a wide range of fabrics on hand when you begin a fabric collage. This vest incorporates vintage and contemporary home-decorative fabrics, hand-woven metallic Indian cottons, Indonesian cotton batiks, quilting cottons, and Mylar on metallic mesh. *(Photo by Jack Deutsch.)*

"Chelsea's New Friends": The loss of a longtime pet inspired this vest's theme. Layers of metallic threads, ribbons, and trims—even metallic dots woven into tulle—add sparkle to the somber color scheme. *(Photo by Jack Deutsch.)*

From now on, think of your fabric purchases as an investment in yourself as an artist. Then when the inspiration strikes you to start a new piece, you won't have to interrupt the creative flow by trekking to a store for the supplies to manifest your vision. I've come to rely on my in-house stash, which includes a large selection of contemporary quilting cottons in many patterns and color families. These are supported by home-decorative textiles with large motifs, by wonderful bits of vintage fabrics and laces from my grandmother's hands, and by short lengths of shiny novelty fabrics.

Choose fabrics with motifs that attract you, even if you have no idea how you'll use them. One creepy crawly hiding in a collaged garden adds whimsy and fantasy to the author's collages and keeps them from becoming too serious. *(Photo by Grey Crawford.)*

THE QUARTER-YARD PRINCIPLE

Doing fiber collage helps you justify and use your stashed fabrics and also lets you indulge in buying more irresistible fabrics—at far less expense. On your next visit to a fabric store, you can pay for 3 yd. of fabric and come home with 12 different pieces, each just a ¼ yard long. You can buy fabrics that intrigue you but that you've never bought before because they were just too bright, shiny, or exotic for the kind of work you've done.

The bulk of my stash is made up of quarter-yards of 100% cotton prints. These vary widely in color and pattern from bright to subdued and from tiny allover prints to oversized motifs. I have lots of my favorite greens that range from bright, lemony spring pastels to the earthy greens of decaying leaves. Batik fabrics fit into almost all my collages, so I store a large selection of these in allover mottled patterns and also those with specific themes such as undersea or leaf patterns. I especially love ikats, so I've brought many of these into my collection.

I find it fun to use novelty fabrics like Joe Boxer prints for a bit of humor and to use so-called juvenile prints that feature jungle animals or giant bugs to romp in my imaginary gardens. I also keep on hand

many small geometric patterns such as tiny plaids and irregular polka dots and stripes to complement the larger, curvy patterns in my stash. To help you understand more about using contrast and variety as you choose fabrics for collage design, see pp. 21-25.

I suggest you resist the temptation to purchase more than quarter-yards of fabrics as you develop your collage stash. Even with such small pieces to work with, I typically have more than half of each piece left over when I've finished my collage. From a quarter-yard piece of fabric, you can even make 6 yd. of bias binding to finish edges, as you will learn in chapter 5.

This personal color wheel was created using snippets of favorite colors from magazines and paint chips glued to manila mailing labels. This exercise will reveal the genuine color preferences of its maker. *(Photo by Grey Crawford.)*

Collecting colors from magazine photos, cata-logs, and brochures from time to time pro-vides the material for creating a collage that reveals authentic color preferences. *(Photo by Grey Crawford.)*

It is more important to have many options from which to choose than to have large amounts of each fabric. This is a new way of thinking if you are used to purchas-ing yards of one fabric for traditional gar-ments and large quilts. But buying small amounts will give you lots of options as you create your collages, and I think you'll have fun taking this new approach to stockpiling fabric.

Of course there are exceptions to the quarter-yard principle. If a fabric really sings out my name and might work well as a lin-ing, I'll purchase 2 yd. However, I don't keep many of these longer lengths on hand because each takes the storage space of 8 quarter-yards. When a fabric has a very large repeat, such as those used for home decoration, I'll purchase enough yardage to provide one full repeat of the design. Generally, ⅓ yd. to ½ yd. will give me plen-ty to work with.

Finding Your Inner Landscape of Color

Color is thrilling to work with and is one of the most effective design elements. It's usually the first thing people respond to when walking into an environment or viewing art. Since it's impossible to have even a few inches of fabric in every possible hue, pattern, and texture, you have to make choices. The more you know about yourself and your preferences, the easier it will be to keep choice-making from being a daunting experience.

Each of us has what I refer to as an inner landscape of color, which I believe is as unique to us as our fingerprints. As an example, one day I was standing at the cutting table of a quilt store with my selection of earth-tone bolts with richly textured designs. I was thinking to myself that I'd never seen such a gorgeous assortment of colors in my life. The woman behind me, who had an equally splendid selection of brilliant, jewel-colored fabrics, looked at my choices and blurted out, "I've never seen such an ugly pile of colors!" Each of us had chosen colors that made our souls sing, and they couldn't have been more different.

COLLECTING YOUR COLORS

It's important that you become aware of your own color landscape. The more self-aware that you become, the more your collages will truly reflect who you are rather than seem to be carbon copies of someone else's work. To help you become more insightful of your unique preferences, observe yourself as you respond to color, whether you're standing in front of the thread counter or checking out this season's offerings in a mail-order catalog. Start collecting samples of the colors you really love—pages of color and texture from magazines, scraps of fabric from a friend's stash, or bits of ribbon from a gift.

At the paint store, pretend you're going to decorate a room just for yourself. Without worrying about practical matters such as how dark the room might look if you choose crimson walls or whether your favorite shade of amethyst will fit in with the rest of the house, pick out sample cards of the color family—such as purples or greens—you'd most like to live with. Then choose your accessory colors from other paint sample cards. Don't even consider whether these are colors you can wear or if they go together or whether anyone else could stand to live in your room.

A Color-Stretching Exercise

Try this exercise to help you stretch your color savvy. Go to a fabric store that has a good selection of home-decorating fabrics. Focus on the colors rather than on the subject of the prints, and find a printed fabric with at least 7 or 8 colors that you're especially drawn to. Look at this fabric for a minute, then look away and name the colors that you recall, like "teal, bright rose, and lavender." Now take a second look at the fabric for what I call the hidden colors. You may find burgundy, brown, taupe, and lime green lurking in tiny amounts.

If you're having trouble seeing the less apparent colors, look for the colored dots printed along the selvage where the manufacturer's name is located. It's not unusual to find 10 to 15 separate colors indicated here for a fabric design that has only 4 or 5 obvious hues.

The next time you buy quarter-yards of fabric, look for these hidden colors to add variety and to enliven your artwork, especially if they are ones you wouldn't have selected otherwise. They may be colors that you really dislike when used alone, but they will add the important sparks of interest that your designs need. You'll find suggestions in chapter 1 that will help you effectively use these colors.

Colored dots printed along the selvage of some fabrics may reveal some surprising colors you hadn't noticed at first glance. *(Photo by Grey Crawford.)*

According to the artist Paul Klee, "One eye sees, the other feels." Make your choices with your feeling eye.

PUTTING YOUR COLORS TOGETHER

As you collect your color samples, put them in a special box or file. Take some time to develop your collection, then one day make some free time and gather your samples, a glue stick, scissors, and a couple of sheets of around until your arrangements please you, overlapping your samples or leaving white space around them. Then glue the pieces in place. The idea is to get your collection together so that you have a visual reminder of your authentic color preferences.

If you've enjoyed this activity, you might wish to repeat it from time to time. As your color awareness increases, you might find you enjoy a wider spectrum. On the other hand, you may discover that you used to make color selections indiscriminately or according to someone else's suggestions and that you really have much more specific personal color preferences.

EXPLORING YOUR COLOR SENSE

Color sense is the imaginative means by which each of us combines colors that satisfy us. Some people have a natural color sense that allows them to use color confidently without formal knowledge of color theory. Their color decisions are made intuitively and would probably be hard for them to explain. If you fall into this category, be grateful, collect fabrics in the colors you are drawn to, and continue to create with confidence.

However, if your lack of intuition of or knowledge about color makes your creative experimentation a trial rather than a joy, I suggest you slowly begin to learn about color theory. Find out whether your community college offers a beginning design class in the art department. This class will

"Chelsea's New Friends": A variety of surface textures is achieved by using coarse metallic mesh, fine tulle with metallic dots, and sheer polyester/metallic ribbon along with more traditional quilting cottons and home-decorating fabrics. *(Photo by Jack Deutsch.)*

sturdy paper. Put on some soothing music and start to pore over your collection.

Your goal is to create a collage that represents your inner color landscape. There are no rules as to how you arrange your collection, since you're the only one who's going to see it. With your scissors, cut off anything you don't like or change the shapes of your scraps. Then lay the pieces out on the sheets of paper, and group related colors or cluster color combinations that you like. Move them include exercises that demonstrate the various qualities of color and will teach you the language of color and as well as design.

If taking a class isn't feasible, check Resources on p. 168 for some books that contain color exercises to get you started. More than anything, learning a little about color theory will increase your awareness of how other artists use color and will help you to become more conscious of your personal color development.

In the meantime, don't let insecurities about color arrest your progress. You'll learn more by working on your own projects and by developing your seeing skills than by any other means. See the sidebar on p. 31 for another suggestion to help you choose fabrics in colors to enliven your collages.

Choosing Fabrics for Variety and Emphasis

Quilting cottons will provide the bulk of your collage stash. But to give your collages visual punch by providing more texture and contrast, consider using some of the fabrics I have listed below.

DECORATOR FABRICS

Some of my most interesting motifs have come from decorator fabrics. I've found swags and bows, columns, animals, and people, as well as a bounty of fruits, leaves, and flowers. Expect chintzes to lose their slick finishes when they're washed. All home-dec fabrics will become softer after they've been laundered.

VINTAGE FABRICS

I love the mellow look of vintage pieces and the velvety frayed edges that old bark cloths and cotton crepes produce. Be on the alert for attractive old draperies, embroidered or printed hankies, aprons, guest towels, and tablecloths at flea markets and yard sales. Parts of faded or stained pieces can be used, and these are the best bargains.

DRY-CLEAN-ONLY FABRICS

Don't automatically bypass dry-clean-only fabrics just because machine-laundering is part of the collage process. You're being warned that these fabrics may wrinkle, shrink, or lose their finish when they're washed, but that's the effect you're after anyway. You'll get delightful results from using bits of lightweight lamés, rayon velvets, and other sumptuous fabrics from the formalwear section of full-service fabric stores. I'll often purchase just an eighth-yard of these fabrics because I use such tiny amounts of them.

TULLES

Tulle is a very fine, hexagonal netting used for bridal and formalwear. I keep a rainbow assortment of tulle to subtly change colors by overlaying them in my collages, as you'll learn in chapter 5. Colored tulle works wonders to tone down, warm up, or cool off a fabric that isn't quite the color you want. Lightweight tulles can be used to cover fabrics that are old and fragile or likely to fray. Tulles with dots and patterns of glued-on glitter are especially fun to use to add subtle sparkle—and they will come through the laundry looking fine.

Fine tulle with woven-in metallic dots does double duty by providing a subtle sparkle while slightly lowering the value of the light motif underneath. *(Photo by Jack Deutsch.)*

A collection of ribbons and trims hangs ready for at-home shopping when a fabric collage is in progress. *(Photo by Grey Crawford.)*

FABRICS WITH WORDS, LETTERS, AND MUSICAL NOTES

The written word can add humor, emphasis, or mystery to your textile story. Look for fabrics that have messages written on them that speak to you. Some prints look like they have writing on them, but the scribbles are meaningless. These fabrics are also useful because they convey the impression of a message while providing an interesting visual texture.

GHOSTS OF WORKSHOPS PAST

Did you ever dye or stamp small fabric samples in a workshop? Spritz bleach on a scrap to find out what "discharge" means? Make a trial quilting block? Or try out your sewing machine's decorative stitches or twin needles on scrap fabric? You probably held on to those experiments thinking they might come in handy someday. Well, their day may have arrived.

REVERSE SIDES OF PRINTS

The quieter values of the reverse side of a print may complement the other fabrics and provide contrast to its own bright side. Sometimes a motif that is heading in the wrong direction or is flying off the edge of your design will work if you flip it over to the reverse side. If the design is a bit too subdued, use fabric pens to highlight the colors you want to emphasize.

METALLIC AND MYLAR FABRICS

Some fascinating metallic and Mylar fabrics wait to be used only in your collages. Textiles that I wouldn't have noticed a decade ago are those that I seek out now. Some look like variegated sequins, but the little disks can't fall off. Others look like golden netting with holes big enough to let other fabrics show through. Keep your eyes and mind wide open for unexpected treasures.

TRIMS AND RIBBONS

I wear a collaged garment as I would a handmade necklace: as an accessory that's the focal point of my whole outfit. Collaged wall hangings can also be jewel-like. One way to get this gemlike effect is by using metallic and iridescent trims and ribbons. When you're in fabric or trim stores, flea markets or bargain centers, go scavenging for unique embellishments. As you select some of the trims listed in the sidebar on the facing page, think contrast: smooth fabrics with textured, three-dimensional ribbons and braid. If you've chosen to make a monochromatic collage, it may border on boring unless you jazz it up with textured trims and eye-catching embellishments.

Preparing and Storing Fabrics

The spoils from your fabric shopping trips can mount up into a daunting pile if you don't have a system for handling them. That's why I'm a believer in storing them immediately. If you are a prewash advocate, nothing I say here is likely to change your habit of washing and ironing. But I'll share the answer to the question I asked my mother after the birth of my first child: Is it necessary to iron all of baby's pajamas? (I guess I was afraid she would wrinkle!) Mom's advice was "it depends on how much work you want to make for yourself."

The high quality of many of today's fabrics and dyes makes it unnecessary to prewash most selections for fabric collage. A slight shrinkage of your collage to create texture is desirable, so shrinkage is a nonissue. If you have an unwashed vintage fabric or a batiked or hand-dyed piece that may have an excess of dye, dampen a bit of it and rub it against a scrap of white muslin. If color rubs off, wash the fabric until the water runs

clear, then soak it for half an hour in a mixture of 2 tablespoons salt dissolved in a quart of water. Next, thoroughly rinse the fabric again and press while it is still slightly damp between white paper towels so that you can check that all of the excess dye is gone. White vinegar is used to set color, too, but it can act as a bleaching agent, so I prefer to use the saltwater method.

When I bring fabrics home, I sort my quarter-yards by color, then fold them into flat bundles about 5 in. by 6 in. and place them like file cards in my wire-basket drawers. Each color family has its own basket. I store fabrics with large motifs and the same themes together in their own baskets. Potential linings—my 2-yd. lengths—go into separate drawers. When I launch a new project, I start with an idea and a piece of fabric that supports that idea, then I check my storage drawers to see what's waiting there.

Wire storage drawers near the design table keep fabrics, sorted by color, within easy reach. *(Photo by Grey Crawford.)*

3

Free-Motion Sewing

Free-motion sewing, for those of you who've never tried it, is done by disengaging your sewing machine's feed dogs, using a presser foot that doesn't quite make contact with the stitch plate of your machine, and using your hands to determine the direction of the cloth as it passes under the needle. It's an exciting way to create a calligraphy of color and sparkle on your collages and quilts in ways you might not have dreamed possible.

I like the term free-motion sewing to describe this technique because it contains the word free, which has to do with liberation, and motion, which has "an inner impulse or inclination" among its definitions. Free-motion sewing will liberate you from sewing each stitch exactly the same as the last as you do in normal sewing. You'll be able to follow the impulse to explore the stitching line that flows from your needle, creating a texture for your collage that is both exciting and a reflection of your personality.

Machine-Quilting with an Attitude

The mechanics of free-motion sewing and machine-quilting are the same; it's your attitude that makes the difference. A conscientious quilter's standards for machine-quilting are as high as those for hand-quilting. Stitches must be equal in length and of a size suitable to the fabric and design of the quilt. As you can well imagine, it takes as much practice to become a skilled machine-quilter as it does to become a skilled knitter.

Perhaps you've put off learning machine-quilting because you feel you don't have the machine-sewing skills to match the quality of the quilt tops you've made. Using free-motion stitching to create a fabric collage will give you practice in quilting with control, while sparing you the frustration that comes if you're a perfectionist.

(Photo opposite by Grey Crawford; photo above by Jack Deutsch.)

If your goal is to become a proficient machine-quilter, you can strive for even stitches while practicing free-motion sewing on your collage. Then when your first attempts result in stitches that are off-kilter, you can congratulate yourself for having created such artistic texture! You may find yourself so intrigued by the results you get when you loosen up that you'll forget about your original aim. At any rate, the more proficient you become at this carefree and forgiving technique, the more confident you'll become as a machine-quilter.

Perhaps you're already an experienced machine-quilter and quite satisfied with your skills. In that case, expressing yourself more creatively in your needlework may be your goal. As you try the more advanced exercises in this chapter, you'll find the old perfectionist rules loosening their grip on you—and you'll see how easy it is to create unique stitching patterns and spontaneous textures.

This Old Machine Is Going to Do What?

Free-motion sewing demands a lot of our sewing machines. It's not like normal sewing, in which you stitch a seam, pause and press, check your pattern instructions, pin another seam, and so on. (The term I've chosen for that kind of sewing is grown-up sewing.) You'll be stitching for long stretches of time without a break, and you'll be stitching rather fast, which builds up friction and heat.

The process will also be generating a surprising amount of lint inside your machine. No matter what kind of machine you have, you will need to pay attention to its maintenance when using this technique. Clean the lint from your machine and lubricate it according to the manufacturer's instructions before each new project and after every three hours of free-motion stitching, unless it needs it sooner. Skipped stitches and breaking threads are the first clues that cleaning and lubrication are needed.

DOES YOUR SEWING MACHINE MEASURE UP?

Let me assure you that you don't need a multithousand-dollar electronic wonder to do free-motion sewing. In fact, a machine that stitches only a straight line may do just fine. I've seen some old, uncomplicated machines do beautiful free-motion stitching in the hands of a patient sewer. While a sophisticated new machine will make the job somewhat easier and give you more options, it can't substitute for the time you need to invest in practicing this technique.

Your sewing machine needs to meet a few basic criteria. First, the machine must allow you adjust the top and bobbin tensions. The top tension will need adjusting when you use certain metallic, rayon, and other novelty threads and when you use the built-in decorative stitches. The bobbin tension will only need to be adjusted if you decide to use heavier novelty threads in the bobbin.

Second, you must be able to disengage or cover the feed dogs. Since your hands will be moving the fabric under the needle, the feed dogs aren't needed for their normal task. Finally, you'll need to be able to stitch steadily on your machine at a relatively high speed for more than 10 minutes without overheating its motor. Free-motion sewing leaves you unencumbered by the starts and stops of normal sewing, so you're likely to sew for long stretches of time.

If you have a newer machine, you'll find it may have features that make free-motion sewing simpler. One of the most useful is the machine's ability to stop stitching in a needle-down position. With this feature, the needle remains in the fabric each time you pause. This eliminates the uneven stitches caused by inadvertently pulling the fabric away from the needle when you start stitching again. Also convenient is the knee-lift lever for the presser foot on some Bernina and Brother machines, which eliminates the need to take your hands off your work to lift the presser foot and move the fabric. When learning to do free-motion sewing, another helpful feature is the half- or quarter-speed button, which allows a machine to automatically stitch at a slower speed.

SOLVING SOME SEWING-MACHINE PROBLEMS

The condition of your machine is more important than its make or model. If, when you're doing traditional sewing, you can stitch only a few minutes before your machine skips a stitch, it may need a thorough cleaning and oiling. If you've been in the habit of cleaning your machine after every project and it still skips, perhaps you're using the wrong size needle for the task. If you haven't had your machine serviced for a while, the timing could be off

and need adjusting. Something as simple as hitting a pin while stitching can throw the timing off.

Skipped stitches could also mean that your top or bobbin tension needs adjusting. Maybe your sewing-machine repairer put the fear of the Sewing-Machine Gremlin into your heart by telling you to never change the tension adjustments on either the top or the bobbin threads of your machine. If so, you need a new repairperson or, less likely, you need a new machine. You can and should be able to change both the top and bobbin tensions to accommodate a wide variety of novelty and decorative threads as well as ordinary sewing threads. You'll find out more about solving tension problems in the section on threads on pp. 132-136.

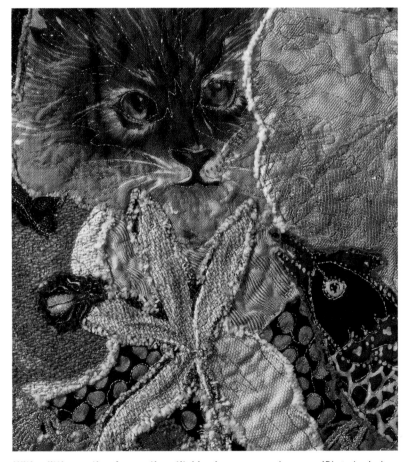

With a little practice, free-motion stitching becomes spontaneous. *(Photo by Jack Deutsch.)*

"All My Senses Sing Her": Free-motion stitching with a graduated zigzag stitch creates the texture in the plain background of this coat. *(Photo by Jack Deutsch.)*

small plate that attaches to the stitch plate to cover the feed dogs. On some older machines, you may simply have to reduce the pressure on the presser foot by turning a knob on the side or top of the machine. In this case, where the feed dogs are still operative, I recommend making a small feed-dog cover out of a piece of plastic template material, an old credit card, or a plastic lid (see the sidebar on the facing page).

Putting the Right Foot Forward

Several presser feet will work for free-motion sewing, depending on your machine. Your manual will probably identify one foot made specifically for darning. Most darning feet are characterized by a small round or rectangular loop that forms the "foot." Some of these feet have an arm with a spring mechanism that rests on the needle clamp, while others have a spring in the shank of the foot. This spring prevents the foot from actually making contact with the bed of the machine during the formation of a stitch and leaves the fabric free to be moved while the needle is in the up position.

Other feet that will also do the job are available. Some sewers prefer a freehand embroidery foot, which looks like a darning foot but has an opening in the front of the loop. Although the visibility is good with this foot, its toes seem to find their way under the loose edges of my collages, so it's not my favorite choice.

A quilting foot is similar to a darning foot, except its metal loop is larger in diameter, allowing better visibility than a small darning foot. However, it's designed to be

PREPARING YOUR MACHINE FOR FREE-MOTION STITCHING

Look up the directions for "darning" in your sewing-machine manual to find out how to set up your particular machine for free-motion stitching. With all machines, you must somehow disengage the feed dogs. Some machines have a switch or button that lowers the feed dogs below the surface of the stitch plate. Others have a

Making a Feed-Dog Cover

To make a feed-dog cover for your sewing machine, cut a rectangular piece of plastic large enough to cover the feed dogs plus about ¼ in. on all sides. This will measure approximately 1 in. by 2 in. Using a utility knife, cut out a small area to expose the hole in your needle plate. If yours is a zigzag machine, make the cut-out area as wide as the hole in the plate so you can use your built-in decorative stitches for free-motion stitching. Align the hole of the plastic cover with the hole in the needle plate, using pressure-sensitive tape to hold the cover in place.

A piece of plastic with a hole to match that in the face plate facilitates free-motion stitching on machines that have stationary feed dogs. *(Photo by Grey Crawford.)*

used with a quilt sandwich that uses batting for its inner layer, which is thicker than the muslin underlining that you'll be using. When you use this foot for fabric collage, it doesn't come down quite as close to the stitch plate, so there is more play or bounce in the fabric as the needle penetrates it. However, I used this foot successfully for a number of years before I returned to using a darning foot, which gave me slightly better control.

My current favorite is a plastic freehand embroidery foot. This small, clear foot gives good visibility as well as good control when stitching. Although this foot was made for use on certain electronic machines that read embroidery patterns, it can also be used on some machines that do not have this feature. Check with your dealer to find out what special-function feet have been designed for your machine.

Many sewers have had great results using a generic Big Foot. It has a clear, concave foot about the size of a quarter. It gives good visibility and control and is available for both high- and low-shank machines. If you decide to use this foot and aren't sure which shank you need, take your normal sewing foot with you when you make your purchase. If you order it from a catalog, measure the length of the shank on your normal sewing foot, and give the make and model of your machine. This foot seems to be the best alternative for older machines whose manufacturers have not provided special feet for free-motion sewing.

From left to right: a generic Big Foot, an open-toed freehand embroidery foot, a plastic freehand embroidery foot, a darning foot, and a quilting foot. These feet have a spring mechanism in common. *(Photo by Grey Crawford.)*

Getting Started on Free-Motion Stitching

I'm going to present several exercises to acquaint you with free-motion sewing before you tackle your collage. If you already have a working knowledge of the technique, you may wish to bypass this section and start stitching on your collage. In that case, turn to the section called "Stitching Techniques to Embellish Your Collage" on p. 50. If you're a confident beginner and balk at samplers and exercises, at least read through these next few pages so you're acquainted with the mechanics of free-motion sewing before you start.

For these exercises, you will need 12 squares of fabric to use to assemble four blocks, or sandwiches, of three layers each. This is a good opportunity to use up odd scraps of muslin or plain, light-colored cotton you couldn't bring yourself to throw out.

1 Begin by cutting out 12 squares of plain fabric, approximately 12 in. by 12 in. each.

2 Assemble four blocks with three layers of fabric each. If you have some cotton flannel, use it for the middle layer. This will eliminate the need to pin or baste the layers

together because the flannel will grab the outer layers, keeping them from shifting. If you use muslin for the inner layer, machine-baste around the outside of each block or use a glue stick or basting spray (see Resources on p. 168) to hold the three layers together.

3 Next, thread your machine and bobbin with a good-quality mercerized cotton or cotton/polyester blended thread, using the top and bobbin tensions you use for normal sewing.

4 After you've threaded the needle, draw the thread through the loop in the darning foot rather than leave it floating above the loop. Any color thread will do; just be sure there is enough contrast so you can really see the stitching on your sample.

ANCHORING THREADS

Whenever possible, begin stitching at the edge of your piece so that it's easy to snip off thread tails. However, when you want to start a new color or rethread in the middle of your piece, the following technique will help you make stitches that won't work loose or get the bobbin thread tangled in your sewing.

1 Start by placing one of your fabric sandwiches under the foot with the needle raised.

2 Lower the presser foot to engage the top tension, holding the tail of the top thread in your left hand while manually turning the handwheel to take one complete stitch in the middle of your sample. Stop with the needle in its highest position.

3 Maintaining tension on the top thread, move the fabric slightly out of the way so that you pull up a little loop of the bobbin thread. Using a pin, pull on the loop to bring it to the surface.

4 Next, hold both threads firmly in your left hand while you move the fabric

STITCH SEQUENCE FOR SECURING THREAD IN THE MIDDLE OF THE WORK

Sewing-machine needle

3   1, 2, 4   5

- When free-motion sewing, your hands will act as a hoop, exerting a slight tension on the fabric around the needle to keep it flat as you stitch. You will be moving too far and too fast to bother with repositioning an actual hoop.

- Your hands will also take the place of the feed-dog and presser-foot action in moving the fabric about under the needle.

- You can stitch in any direction without turning the fabric when doing free-motion sewing. This is very different from using a regular presser foot with the feed dogs engaged. To change the direction of stitching when doing normal sewing, you must stop the machine, put the needle in the down position, raise the presser foot, reorient the fabric in the new direction you want to sew, lower the presser foot, and stitch until you want to change direction again. When you're doing free-

motion sewing, just the movement of your hands will determine the direction the fabric moves. That's where the free in free motion comes in and the fun begins.

- The length of your stitches will depend on how fast you run the machine and how rapidly you move your hands. There's no need to set the stitch-length adjustment, since it now has no effect.

- The presser foot must always be in the down position when stitching. Otherwise, the tension will not be engaged, and you'll end up with a tangle of threads when you begin. (With certain Pfaff machines, the foot must be in the special darning position. Check your owner's manual.)

- The feed dogs must be disengaged or covered, although I confess that I have occasionally forgotten this step and not had a problem. Not all machines may be so forgiving!

back to its original position so you can make two stitches in the same hole where you brought up the bobbin thread. Then move the fabric back slightly to take one stitch behind the first stitches (see the illustration on the facing page).

5 Take another stitch in the original hole, and you're ready to take off stitching. Once you've stitched a couple of inches away from these anchoring stitches, clip both thread tails close to the fabric.

Making these tiny back-and-forth stitches requires a conscious effort at first, but with a little practice you'll soon be anchoring your threads automatically. This method creates a less detectable and more reliable thread anchor than the usual method of making five or six stitches in place, which leaves a long knot on the underside that often works itself loose.

CONVERTING HANDS TO HOOPS
This next exercise will help you get a feel of the hand position you need for free-motion stitching.

1 Place your hands on the sewing table of your machine with one of your fabric sandwiches between your fingers and the table (see the photo below).

*Practicing the "motion" of free-motion stitching before using your sewing machine helps to develop good technique.
(Photo by Grey Crawford.)*

2 Notice that your two pointer fingers and thumbs form the "hoop" that will control how your fabric moves. The other three fingers on each hand should rest comfortably in a slightly curved position. Rest the heels of your hands lightly on the surface of the fabric, or raise them slightly in a piano-player position. You will need to experiment to find your most comfortable, relaxed position.

3 Next, visualize the scrolls you made when you were first practicing cursive writing. With both hands in the stitching position, move them together in loops like those imaginary scroll paths. This is how your hands are going to manipulate the fabric when it's under the needle and your foot is on the control.

WARMING UP

If you have a newer sewing machine with a half-speed control, engage it before you begin this warming-up exercise. Ultimately, you'll want to stitch at a faster speed, as that will make it easier to regulate your stitches. For now, however, you need to develop a sense of working in rhythm with your machine. This will be easier if you can floor your foot control without going so fast that you lose control.

1 Begin by placing your fabric sandwich under the needle so that you can sew from the left edge to the right. Lower the presser foot to engage the top tension so you won't end up with a tangle of loops on the underside of your stitches.

2 Before you start sewing, hold the top and bobbin threads firmly in your left hand, even if you are beginning at the edge of the fabric. If you don't, you'll create a nest of threads on the back of your work as you sew.

3 Position your hands with your two pointer fingers slightly behind the needle and about 2 in. on either side of it. Your thumbs should be close together and in front of the needle.

4 Start stitching, moving your fabric in the scrolling pattern you just practiced. If your machine doesn't have a half-speed control, try to maintain a steady, medium speed rather than speeding up and suddenly slowing down. Keep your fingers in firm contact with your work, but don't use more pressure than necessary to keep the fabric moving. Using too much pressure is not only tiring but also is likely to cause jerky movements.

5 Until you get a feel for the movement of the fabric under the needle, keep stitching scrolls. You'll see a wonderful pattern of stitches flowing from the needle like a fine pencil line (see the photo below).

Start free-motion stitching by making scrolls. *(Photo by Grey Crawford.)*

Reducing Stress

Pay attention to your body position. If your shoulders are hiked up to your ears and your arms are pressed into your sides, you'll soon be exhausted. Relax! You'll need to remind your body to do this; otherwise it will stay in tense mode. Gently telling your shoulders to stay down will help. A good chair that can be raised so that you are looking slightly down on your work will help, too.

Try these simple relaxing tricks.

• Gently lower your chin to your chest, then slowly rotate your head to the right until your right ear is aligned with your right shoulder. Let your head rest in this posi-tion for a moment, then slowly rotate your head forward again, passing your chin across your chest and bringing your left ear into alignment with your left shoulder. Repeat this exercise slowly several times, always rolling your head forward.

• Lift your shoulders up and try to touch them to your ears. Contract your shoulder, neck, and upper arm muscles, and hold them tight while you count to 10. Slowly lower your shoulders. At the same time, flex your hands, and push your palms down as far as they will go while you count to 10.

CONTROLLING THE SIZE OF STITCHES

When you can comfortably sew a scrolling pattern and maintain a steady sewing speed, you're ready to try this next exercise in controlling the size of your stitches. If you've engaged the half-speed control, disengage it for this exercise. If your machine has a needle-down option, select it now.

1 Place the second fabric sandwich under the foot, and prepare to sew from the top left-hand corner. You'll be stitching in straight lines from the top to the bottom of your sample.

2 Starting with a slow machine speed, use your hands to slowly move the fabric away from you. Note the length of your stitches; they should be quite short.

3 Sew a second line of stitches next to the first, beginning with the same slow machine speed, then gradually increasing the speed at which you move the fabric. Notice that the stitches turn into long basting stitches.

4 For your third row of stitches, increase your sewing-machine speed while moving the fabric slowly once again. Your stitches should be very tiny. When you work with a rapid needle speed and slow-moving fabric, you must take care that the stitches don't pile up so that you can't move the fabric at all.

If this does happen, use the handwheel to raise the needle to its highest position and also raise the presser foot. Lift the fabric penetrated by the needle as high as you can, exposing the knotted bundle of stitches on the underside. Then use small, sharp scissors to snip through them. You'll need to remove your fabric—and possibly the needle plate—to thoroughly clean out the rest of the snipped threads before you rethread the machine.

5 Sew your last row of stitches at a faster speed. Try to form stitches that are even and close to a normal sewing length. With more practice, you'll be able to change the length of your stitches at will.

6 On the remaining space of this sample, practice gradually changing the speed of your machine from slow to fast. At the same time, move the fabric at varying speeds to create a meandering line of stitches of varying lengths. Notice how this variety in stitch length alone changes the character of the line you're creating.

SEWING TO, FRO, AND SIDEWAYS

When you do free-motion sewing, you don't need to rotate your fabric to change the direction of stitching except to rearrange a large piece of work for easier handling. To make a right-angle turn from a line of stitches that's heading toward you, you just shift mental gears and sew sideways—a notion that takes a little getting used to, as conventional sewing doesn't give us this option.

1 Use your third 12-in. block to practice changing the direction of your stitching line. Look at the sewing paths shown in the photo below.

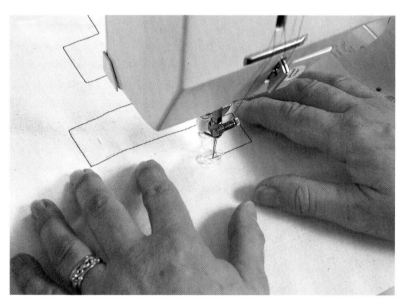

With a little practice, you'll learn to sew with precision in any direction without turning the cloth. *(Photo by Grey Crawford.)*

2 Starting at the middle of the top edge, duplicate those sewing paths by stitching forward then sideways, first moving your fabric away from you then straight to the side without turning it.

3 Next, stitch forward again, this time moving the fabric sideways in the opposite direction. Do this slowly until you feel comfortable, then increase your speed while you draw a pattern of overlapping right angles and diagonal lines over your sample.

You'll soon get the feel for moving your fabric in time with your machine. Pay attention with your fingertips as to how smoothly the fabric slides as you move it. If you sense that your threads are bunching up on the underside, immediately stop and free it. If you tug at jammed fabric while stitching, you can pull the needle off track so that it strikes the needle plate or foot, causing the needle to bend or break.

Keep your eyes focused on the area of the fabric you're stitching toward so you can make decisions about the path you take. Free-motion sewing is almost like riding a bike. If you focus on the front wheel, you'll wobble all over and hit the stone that makes you tumble. On the other hand, keeping your eyes on the road just ahead helps you stay on the path, and you can stop if you need time to make a decision on where to go next.

ZIGZAGGING AND BEYOND

Most machines—mechanical and electronic—offer a zigzag stitch and at least a few other stitch-pattern options. If your machine does, use your fourth sample block to experiment with some of those stitches to discover other ways to give your stitch lines character.

1 Begin by selecting the zigzag stitch and setting the stitch-width control between 2.5mm and 3mm. As you stitch forward,

The character of line changes as you switch from a narrow zigzag to a wide zigzag and then to an ogive stitch with free-motion sewing. Note that the ogive stitch on the right begins as a single stitch, becomes an increasingly wider zigzag stitch, then returns to a single stitch. *(Photo by Grey Crawford.)*

Exploring Your Machine's Built-In Stitches

If your machine offers a variety of built-in stitches, try using some of them for free-motion sewing. Keep in mind that the stitches that incorporate reverse stitching, such as the feather stitch, display their reverse stitches only when the feed dogs and the presser foot are engaged. You may find it more satisfying to use the stitches designed to move forward only. My favorites are the serpentine and ogive (or satin-stitched leaf) stitches, as they create such surprising patterns and thick and thin lines as I move my fabric under the needle.

increase then decrease the rate at which you move the fabric. You'll notice that doing so has the same effect as adjusting the stitch-length control in conventional sewing.

2 Next, gradually move the fabric diagonally then sideways to the left or right, and watch the line become straight again, even though the machine is still forming a zigzag stitch.

3 Continue to experiment, changing the width of the stitch as well as the direction and speed of your stitching, just to familiarize yourself with the possibilities that lie in this common stitch.

VARYING STITCHED-LINE WIDTHS

You can also vary the width of your stitched lines just as an artist uses variety in the thickness, or weight, of a pencil line to create interest. To explore this technique, prepare a three-layer sample block as before, this time using a fabric with a large-scale motif, such as a drapery fabric, for the top layer. Choose any thread that contrasts with your fabric so you'll be able to see your stitches.

You'll soon be able to enhance any design with free-motion outlining. It's not necessary to follow the design precisely; let the stitches flow from your sewing machine like a pencil line. *(Photo by Grey Crawford.)*

1 Set your machine to do a straight stitch and practice outlining part of the design (see the photo above). Stop with your needle in the fabric and look at your stitches. You may have missed the edge of your design in a few places.

2 Without repositioning your fabric, sew backward over the same path. Let your line sometimes meet the previous line of stitching and other times wander beside it.

If your machine offers more than straight stitching, try these techniques.

• *Select the zigzag mode, and set the stitch width at 2mm to 2.5mm (medium wide).* Use this stitch to follow the edge of a motif, then let it meander through an open area of the design. You can move the fabric forward, diagonally, and sideways to create thick and thin lines. Unless your machine has a self-adjusting tension, you may need to loosen the upper tension to prevent drag on the thread. You'll know the upper thread tension is too tight if you see loops of the bobbin thread on the top of your sewing. Loosen the tension in small increments, checking each time you make a change to see if it is balanced.

Use stitching to highlight images in the collage. *(Photo by Jack Deutsch.)*

• *Reset your machine to do a dense satin-stitch pattern such as the ogive or shell stitch.* Let your stitches wander about the patterned sampler. Is there a place in the design that strikes you as particularly interesting when stitched this way? I use this technique to embellish plain fabric that has little or no pattern. The irregular texture created by using these stitches also contrasts nicely with shiny fabrics such as taffeta or lamé.

Relax! Give yourself plenty of time to play with what you're learning.

• *Try the same meandering stitching with the serpentine stitch (sometimes called a running or continuous-zigzag stitch).* The effect of using a wandering single line of stitching like this one is very different from the effect you get using a dense stitch—there are no thick and thin lines. Instead you will have a single line of stitches with a mind of its own.

• *On an unstitched area, use the normal straight stitch, and try repeating some simple freehand designs such as stars or spirals.* You don't have to stop between motifs;

"What a Fruitful Year": The name of this vest became part of the surface design. A washable marker was used to write the message, then free-motion stitching was used to trace over the words several times with two values of the same color of rayon thread. *(Photo by Jack Deutsch.)*

just stitch to another spot and doodle another design. Each time you do this, it'll become a little easier. When you've covered an area with these designs, the variety (and even the irregularity) will work together to create a pleasing texture.

• *To make your collages more intriguing, sew words onto them.* Practice writing the letters most familiar to you—your signature. You'll soon be able to write anything you wish in your own style—without a built-in automatic alphabet. Don't bother to dot i's and j's.

• *Relax!* Give yourself plenty of time to play with what you're learning.

3 Next, stitch back and forth several times for a distance of 1 in. to 2 in. to give more weight to your line. This kind of line, meeting itself and wandering away again, has wonderful character! To learn more about your machine's capacity to create intriguing texture with ordinary stitches, try some of the ideas suggested in the sidebar on the facing page.

Using Novelty Threads

Now that you've seen how to add character to your collaged quilts by changing the line of stitching you use, you're ready to learn how to add color, sparkle, and luster to your designs with novelty threads. You've probably noticed that there are lots of irresistible threads being used by machine-quilters and artwear designers. These vary from fine rayon and ribbonlike metallic threads to heavier twisted cords and even narrow silk ribbons.

The availability of different types of decorative threads vary from one section of the country to another. You may live in an area where you are totally dependent on mail-order resources. In any case, I recommend that you begin by using threads that are readily available to you. Buy a spool, experiment using the following suggestions, then keep track of the results so you'll know just what to do the next time you want to use that thread.

I've experimented with just about every thread that's available in my area, including some imported novelties I found in the fishermen's fly-tying store down the road. By experimenting, I've been able to use almost every thread I've tried.

Among novelty threads, rayon threads are perhaps the easiest to use, although they aren't as strong as normal cotton or cotton/polyester sewing thread. Rayon threads are lustrous and add a subtle sheen to the surface of collage.

Metallic threads are of two types. The first has a metallic filament spun around a core of nylon or other synthetic. YLI calls this Fine Metallic, Sulky refers to it as Metallic, and Madeira calls it Japan Threads. I refer to all of these threads as "metallic." They seem to offer the greatest challenge to sewers because they tend to fray so easily.

The second metallic thread is a shiny, narrow, flat ribbon of aluminum-coated polyester, sometimes referred to as Mylar thread. This type of thread offers the most sparkle for the buck. Sulky distributes this type of thread under the name Sliver, and Coats calls theirs Glitz. Madeira's Jewel and GlissenGloss's Prizm are similar but have a prismatic or holographic surface.

All of these threads can be used either through the needle or in the bobbin. When

The ogive stitch creates an interesting thick-and-thin line when combined with free-motion stitching. *(Photo by Grey Crawford.)*

(Photo by Grey Crawford.)

you're first experimenting with any of these through the needle, I suggest using cotton/polyester thread in the bobbin because it's durable and dependable. Then when you've gained some confidence in using novelty threads, try using them in different combinations both through the needle and in the bobbin.

There are several factors that will help you use decorative threads successfully. First, use a needle made especially for use with metallic threads. These will have "met" in their names: Metafil and Metallica are two that I've used. They have a deeper scarf, or groove, to carry the thread and a longer eye than ordinary needles. Both of these features reduce friction, which causes shredding, as the thread progresses through the needle.

A collaged sampler using a variety of thread types becomes the focal point of a pillow. (Photo by Jack Deutsch.)

I've found that it's a nuisance to switch back and forth between different needles each time I change the type of thread I'm using to embellish my collages. In an innocent act of rebellion, I decided to try using a size 80/12 Metalfil or Metallica needle with all of my rayon, metallic, and Mylar-type threads. I sometimes leave it on my machine when I am doing normal clothing construction. You might want to try this, too, but don't tell anyone that I told you to! An alternative to these special needles for metallic threads is to use topstitch needles, which are available in sizes 80, 90, and 100, which has the largest needle eye.

A second aid to reduce friction is the use of a silicone lubricant such as Sewers Aid. Contact your sewing-machine dealer and manufacturer for their recommendations for using lubricants. Misuse on some machines may cause deterioration of the tension disks or other machine parts. I put a drop of

lubricant on the tiny trough that guides the thread after it goes through the tension disks on my machine, then I reapply as needed, about every half hour of sewing.

My third suggestion when using novelty threads is to loosen the top tension slightly. All of these suggestions will reduce friction on the thread as it goes through your sewing machine on its way to embellishing your collage. If your thread still frays, see pp. 132-136 for suggestions on how to use decorative threads in the bobbin, then stitch from the back side of your collage so the bobbin thread will end up where you want it.

Stitching Techniques to Embellish Your Collage

You are now ready to start stitching on your collage! Believe me, this project becomes more fun with each step. If you are feeling insecure about which thread to use, select one that is cotton or cotton/polyester in a color that blends with the midvalue colors that dominate your collage. For the bobbin thread, choose the same type of thread in a color to blend with the backing.

Another safe choice is variegated thread. Choose one in colors that are compatible with those in your collage. The advantage of using a variegated thread is that it will look like you have changed the bobbin thread without the effort of doing so. Sometimes I use just one variegated rayon thread in the bobbin to embellish the entire collage.

Notice that I emphasize using compatible colors rather than matching colors. Matching thread color to a collage is nearly impossible and not nearly as interesting as having compatible colors that enhance the visual texture you are creating. If you're having trouble letting go of the grown-up sewing concept of having thread color match fabric color, think of meadows, gardens, and forests. They'd look so boring if all of their greens matched. Instead, they keep us coming back for another look because we're intrigued by the sage, verdigris, chartreuse, and myriad other related greens that we see.

USING LEFTOVER THREADS

When I first started making collages and realized that I was using four or five spools of thread on each vest I created, I decided it was a good time to empty the partially used spools and bobbins that were taking up precious space in my thread cabinet. I learned a lot about stitching with colors of thread that didn't match my fabrics by observing the results of my spool-emptying exercise. The most important thing I learned was that the more my thread color contrasted to the color of the fabrics I was sewing on, the more significant my stitches became as a design element.

Another thing I learned was that a little line of stitching was just that—a little line of stitching. Therefore I couldn't choose a color that was wrong as long as I chose something I liked. I also made the happy discovery that an abundance of free-motion sewing created a sumptuous texture that helped unify the surface and the design of my collages.

EMBELLISHING YOUR COLLAGE WITH STITCHES

The first step in stitching on your collage is to remove the pins that hold the sandwich together. Set up your machine for free-motion stitching, remembering to disengage or cover the feed dogs, to use a darning or free-motion embroidery foot, and to lower the foot to employ the tension. Use the needle-down position if your machine is computerized, then set your machine for straight stitching and begin stitching at one edge of your collage.

Hold the thread tails for the first several stitches to avoid creating a bothersome tangle of threads on the underside of your work. Then meander around the collage

"Friendly Encounter": Iridescent threads, which are used in the bobbin, and textile paint transform the cotton batik lining of this swing coat. *(Photo by Jack Deutsch.)*

from pin to pin, in the same manner in which you'd play the Connect the Dots game, removing the pins as you come to them. Don't stitch over the pins, as that's an invitation to break a needle or throw off your machine's timing.

If this is your first free-motion project, stitch through the middle of the motifs and background fabrics instead of trying to stitch along the raw edges as you go from pin to pin. Just getting rid of the pins at this stage will make it easier to handle the fabric and stitch along the raw edges later.

Once all the pins are removed, the machine-embellishment process gets a lot easier—and more fun. If you are

Remove pins as you go to avoid stitching over them. *(Photo by Grey Crawford.)*

Choose bobbin thread in a midvalue of the predominant color of the lining to blend it into the background. For an exciting, dramatic effect, select a high-contrast thread or a shiny metallic one. *(Photo by Grey Crawford.)*

Metallic threads highlight the birds gathering on this collage. Notice how the style of stitching changes from one fabric to the next. *(Photo by Jack Deutsch.)*

a free-motion sewing novice and have done the exercises suggested earlier in the chapter, you have a chance to perfect your new skills as you embellish your collage. As you gain self-confidence, you will be able to stitch faster and more spontaneously. If you are already an accomplished free-motion stitcher, this is your opportunity to build on what you already know.

As you hone your skills, you will be able to consider what is happening on the bobbin side of your work at the same time you are paying attention to the effects of stitching on the surface of your collage. If your machine and threads are up to it, you may find yourself sewing "pedal to the metal" and loving the exhilaration of the experience. Just be careful not to go too fast, or you may find some of the more fragile metallic threads shredding. In that case you'll have to stop and rethread the machine, and that part isn't fun.

TENDING THE RAW EDGES

After each piece of your collage is anchored with stitches, it's time to pay attention to the raw edges on your motifs and background fabrics. Stitching ⅛ in. from the edges of most quilting cottons will hold them in place and leave a good margin for fraying without having the fabric pull away from the stitching. On some heavier home-decorative fabrics, stitching 3/16 in. from the edge will allow for more fraying to create a rich, velvety edge.

On lightweight fabrics like silk, on fabrics that fray easily like lamé, and on the ends of synthetic ribbons, two or three rows of tiny stitches placed side by side about ⅛ in. from the raw edges will help keep the fabric from pulling away from the stitching during laundering. As a rule of thumb, you can stitch closer to the edges of tightly woven fabrics that don't fray easily. You can also stitch closer to the edges when you use tiny stitches that won't pull out easily.

DEVELOPING YOUR OWN STITCHING STYLE

In addition to stitching along the raw edges, stitch through the centers of your motifs and background fabrics. This can be done in a number of ways. If a motif has some detail such as leaves, fruit, or birds, consider creating a calligraphy of stitching in a contrasting color or metallic thread to highlight them.

Calligraphy means the art of fine hand-writing, but when used as an art term, it refers to any line that resembles hand-writing. A watercolorist may use a pen or very fine brush to go back over a wash of color to give a painting definition. In the same way, a sewing-machine artist can use a line of contrasting stitching to give fabric designs definition.

As you develop your free-motion sewing techniques, this stitching will become as personal as your handwritten signature. If you decide to do a calligraphic style of stitching on a particular motif, be consistent and stitch in the same way on several more of these motifs scattered about your collage. This will help to unify the artwork. It isn't necessary that you stitch in the same way every time you come to that motif. But just as I suggested that you use a motif or back-ground fabric at least three times to create unity by repetition, you'll create a more harmonious piece by repeating the stitching styles throughout your collage.

STITCHING WITH THE DESIGN

Another way to stitch the surface of your collage is to mimic the lines of the designs printed on the fabrics. This might mean doing successive rows of straight stitching in a random fashion on plaid fabrics, or it might mean freely repeating flower outlines on another fabric. It isn't necessary to precisely follow the lines; in fact, it's more interesting if you are more casual about following them.

The author's style of stipple stitching departs from the traditional. Notice how the braided trim indicates the flight path of the bee. *(Photo by Jack Deutsch.)*

It's also fun to repeat a printed design by stitching it in a different scale. On one project, I used metallic thread to free-motion stitch large stars on top of a fabric printed with tiny, gold metallic stars. I use this same technique when I emphasize polka-dotted fabric by stitching random loops around and between the dots.

STIPPLE STITCHING

A decade ago, stipple stitching became quite popular among some machine-quilters. Strictly defined, stippling is a continuous, meandering line of stitches that never crosses back over itself. It takes some skill to perfect the technique of free-motion stippling, so those quilters who would like to become proficient at it will find that collage is the perfect place to practice.

The stipple stitch has become so appeal-ing that some new sewing machines include it in their repertoire of built-in stitches. If your machine has this feature, experiment with the automatic stipple stitch as you develop your free-motion skills. If you do happen to cross over one of your stitching lines, no one is likely to notice. My own particular style of stipple stitching is very casual, and I purposely meander back over my stitched lines. Using the continuous

Echo stitching creates a wonderful textured surface on a plain background fabric. *(Photo by Jack Deutsch.)*

Echo quilting repeats the edge of a motif. In traditional sewing, the lines of stitching are equidistant, but that's not necessary in free-motion sewing.

zigzag, or serpentine, stitch also creates an erratic stipple effect that is very interesting.

ECHO QUILTING

Echo quilting is also popular among both hand- and machine-quilters. Echo quilting repeats the edge of a motif like the ripples around a pebble dropped into water. Traditionally, each row of echo stitching is equidistant from the last. When I do echo stitching, however, I strive for a less formal effect. To do this, I straight-stitch lines that wander close together then separate again (see the illustration above). I often do this

style of free-motion stitching on large areas of plain fabric such as on the vest in the photo above.

Another striking effect is achieved by using one of the decorative stitches from the exercises on p. 48 to do a meandering echo stitch. This fills an open area relatively quickly and creates an interesting texture at the same time.

SWITCHING THREAD COLORS

When you want to use more than one thread color, stitch over the entire surface of your collage with one color before changing to another. For instance, if you have five purple elephants trailing across your piece and want them embellished with silver loops of thread, do some of the loops on at least three of them before deciding whether you want the whole herd to look the same way. If so, do the other two, then

Assessing Your Work

It's a good idea to stop sewing every half hour to rest your body and give it a few moments' attention. That will also give you an opportunity to stand back and assess your work. Ask yourself the following questions.

• *Am I getting an even amount of stitching all over the collage, or am I overworking some areas?* Too much stitching in one spot will keep the fabric from shrinking evenly. It's better to err on the side of too little stitching rather than too much. It's much easier to add stitches than to take them out.

• *Do I have a good balance between stitches that draw attention to themselves and those that are less obvious?* Stitching that's done with a thread color that's in high contrast to the fabric color, such as burgundy metallic thread on a soft mauve background fabric, will draw more attention to itself. Such stitching can help balance a motif that is otherwise overpowering.

• *Are there any areas that I've neglected to stitch as I get close to finishing the free-motion stitching?* Looking at the back side of your collage will help you find the forgotten areas.

• *Am I stitching back far enough from the raw edges so that they won't pull out when they're laundered?* If you miss edges or if they pull away from the stitching when you gently tug on the fabric, go back with another row of stitching inside of the faulty one. You don't have to match thread color to that of the previous row of stitching.

• *Are my free-motion sewing skills improving?* You bet they are!

Metallic thread embellishes the parrots and relates them to the accent of metallic fabric. Bits of metallic stitching also winds its way through the background, which is mostly stitched with rayon thread. *(Photo by Jack Deutsch.)*

look for other places you would like to stitch with the same silver thread. When you feel there's enough silver stitching, switch to a thread of another color and repeat the process.

Your collage can't help but be beautiful if you take time as you sew to be mindful of what is happening on it. Pause at regular intervals to observe what you've done.

You'll know when you're finished because your collage will look and feel as if it has a uniform amount of stitching all over it. No matter how much fun you're having sewing, remember that the more you stitch, the stiffer your collage will become, so don't overdo it.

4

Basic Finishing Techniques

At this point in your project, you have a textured fabric collage that may remind you of a beginner's sewing project. Now you're going to transform those humble beginnings into a respectable piece of artwork—by doing laundry.

It All Comes Out in the Wash

Washing your collage is when the magic takes place. To soften the fibers and the raw edges of your collage, set your washing machine for a normal wash cycle and use a nonbleaching soap. I use Orvus paste, a cleaning product developed by animal caretakers that's been adopted by quilt caretakers. It removes sizing and softens the fabric without stripping fibers of their luster. I use about a tablespoon of the paste in a normal-sized laundry load. In its

absence, your regular laundry product will do. Just don't use one that contains bleach unless you want your collage's colors to soften considerably.

I also add my regular fabric softener to the rinse water, as I usually wash my collages with the household laundry. So far none of the many collages I've made have suffered from such humble treatment. On the rare occasions when I'm caught up with the household laundry, I wash my collage with several clean towels, which provide the necessary abrasion. I use small-load settings, a teaspoon of Orvus paste, and a wash cycle of three or four minutes—and the effect is the same as washing it with my husband's running clothes. Don't be too shocked and dismayed when you see all the frayed edges and loose threads dangling from your damp collage: They'll be dealt with before you're finished.

A shaggy, wet collage goes for a spin in the dryer. (Photo by Grey Crawford.)

USING YOUR DRYER

The next step will be a challenge for readers schooled in the fine points of couture sewing. Drying the collage in a dryer, not on a line, is an important part of the process. It takes the heat of a dryer to uniformly shrink the various collage fabrics, threads, and backing fabric. Using a dryer also fluffs up the piece's raw edges that frayed in the washing machine.

To dry your collage, place it in the dryer along with towels or the rest of your laundry. Use a normal heat setting unless you've used a fabric or thread that comes with a heat-caution label. In that case, use a lower heat setting and dry the collage slowly. I've used all of the novelty threads mentioned in chapter 3 and haven't had a problem with any of them melting in my dryer. If you're in doubt about any of the threads you've used, make a test sample and toss it in your next load of laundry before you launder your collage. Give your samples the toughest treatment they are likely to receive so you won't have unexpected surprises with your finished collages.

When you take your collage out of the dryer, you'll be amazed at the change in its appearance. The soft texture created by the puckers will unify the collage into a harmonious whole. Now, any misgivings you may have had about your collage "working" should vanish.

Dark fabrics, particularly ones that aren't printed or embellished with a contrasting thread, will be more likely to show the effects of the dryer's abrasion, just as dark clothing is likely to show the wearing effects of being put through normal laundering. I personally like this softening effect on my collages, but if you want yours to stay as bright as possible, wash your collage with cold water using no soap or detergent, and set your machine on the shortest wash cycle. Tumble-dry for about five minutes to give the raw edges a chance to fray and the threads a chance to shrink, then finish by air-drying before you proceed (although I'm usually not that patient).

Shaping Up the Collage

Once your collage has been laundered, it's time to shape it up. To do so, spread it on a cutting mat and hand-press it as smooth and as flat as you can. In the lifetime of your collage, never use an iron to press it, as that will remove all the puckers and fluffy edges you've been working for.

After the collage emerges from the washing and drying process, its soft allover texture unifies its separate parts. The collage is ready to have its edges squared and trimmed even. (Photo by Grey Crawford.)

If your collage is a rectangle, square it by lining up one of its long sides with a gridline on your cutting mat, then trim off the uneven edges with a rotary cutter. Make sure you are removing enough of the raw edges to leave them clean on both the collaged side and the backing side. Repeat with the other three sides.

If your collage is a circle or an irregular shape that you've made from a paper pattern, lay the pattern on top of the collage and hold it in place with weights before you cut the collage to size. Depending on the collage's shape, you may be able to trim the edges freehand with either scissors or a rotary cutter.

Finishing the Edges: A Nontraditional Approach

The edges of a quilt are typically bound with straight-grain or bias strips. Many traditional quilt books have good instructions for this kind of finish (I've listed several of them in the Resources on p. 168). These bound edges are perfectly fine for your collage, however, you may want to try an edging I've developed that's based on traditional piping and facing. This technique gives a neat finish to the outer edge of the collage but has a softer look that's more in keeping with the collage's surface.

"Sunshine on My Shoulder": A triangle-shaped facing that's in a high-contrast color to the collage makes a bold statement and becomes an important design element on the finished collage. *(Photo by Jack Deutsch.)*

In brief, this edging is a small, corded piping made by sewing a bias fabric strip over nylon drapery cord. The piping is applied to the raw edges of the collage, then the edges are faced with triangles of fabric that are overlapped and sewn together to form a continuous chain.

When selecting the fabric to make the piping and the facing for your collage, consider that they will have the same effect as a small frame and a jagged mat on a picture. The fabrics you choose should make a statement that says, "The collage stops here." You may want to make the statement boldly, such as by using a triangle facing made from fabric in one of the accent colors in your collage. Such an edging would be prominent and draw attention to itself

By the Way

Washers from the hardware store make wonderful, economical weights for holding patterns in place when cutting out projects with a rotary cutter. I keep a basket, with washers ranging in size from 1½ in. to 2¾ in., near my cutting table for use in all my sewing projects.

and to the accent color in the artwork. The piping used with such a facing can blend in with the facing or it can be in high contrast to it.

A more subtle approach would be to select fabric in a complementary color that is slightly lighter or darker than the predominant colors in the collage. Such a piping with lower contrast would also make a statement that the piece is finished but without shouting it out.

MAKING THE CORDED PIPING

To make the piping, use nylon or Dacron drapery cord, which gives a firm surface to sew against, unlike cotton/polyester cord. I use the Conso cording that is sold in drapery shops because it won't shrink. Some drapery cords do shrink, and using them will give a puckered, distorted edge to your collage. If you buy another brand of drapery cord, wash it by hand in very hot water and dry it in the dryer before using it. Or put the cord in the toe of a stocking, tie the stocking shut, and wash and dry it with a regular load of laundry.

You will need the following materials for corded piping:

- A zipper foot or piping foot
- 2mm nylon drapery cord, in a length that equals the measurement of the outside edges of your collage plus 6 in.
- ¼ yd. fabric
- A rotary cutter and board
- An 18-in. clear acrylic ruler

Selecting a midvalue color for the facing is a subtler (and safer) effect. Whether you choose to finish your collage with a bold statement or a subtle one is not a better-or-worse issue: It's simply a choice. *(Photo by Jack Deutsch.)*

By the Way

When making bias strips for piping or binding, it's not necessary to cut on the true bias of the fabric. True bias is a 45-degree angle from the straight grain (or the selvage edge) of the fabric. It is only necessary to have the bias enough off-grain so that it has give and can be stitched smoothly around soft curves. Bias strips that are cut on a 30-degree angle will give sufficient flexibility for all of the projects in this book. A quarter-yard of fabric will provide 6 yd. or more of pieced bias strips, depending on the width of the fabric.

Use a rotary cutter to make your first diagonal cut. *(Photo by Grey Crawford.)*

Measure and cut 1¼-in. strips from your doubled fabric. *(Photo by Grey Crawford.)*

To make bias strips, take a quarter-yard of fabric and lay a clear 18-in. ruler across it so that the point of the ruler's top edge lies near the top center of the fabric. Then position the ruler so the point of its lower edge touches the lower edge of the fabric, and make your first diagonal cut with a rotary cutter (see the above left photo).

Flip the left piece of fabric over, and position it on top of the right piece, perfectly aligning their two diagonal edges. Next, use the ruler to measure and cut 1¼-in. strips from your doubled fabric (see the above right photo). Each time you make a cut, you will have a 1-yd. bias strip. Five cuts will provide you with enough strips to piece together 5 yd. of bias binding.

When you sew together the short strips of fabric to make a long bias strip to cover the cord, sew their angled ends right sides together, as shown in the illustration at right. This maintains the flexibility of the bias. Sew strips together until their measurement equals the distance around your collage plus about 6 in., then finger-press the seams open.

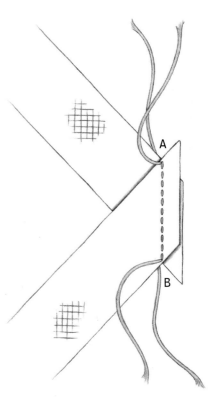

Match the straight-grain cut edges of the bias strips with right sides together. Offset the straight edges to form Vs at A and B, then stitch to join the points of the Vs.

To keep the piping straight and taut, position one hand slightly behind the rotary cutter when trimming the piping's seam allowance. *(Photo by Grey Crawford.)*

EMPTYING THE PIPING ENDS

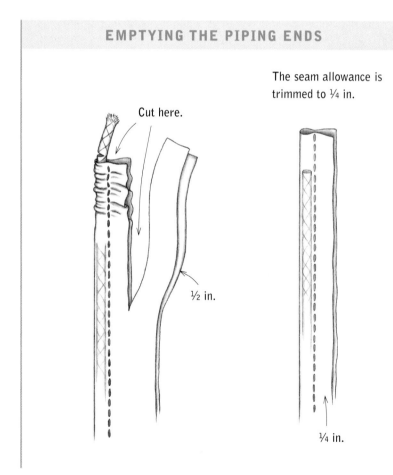

Cut here.

The seam allowance is trimmed to ¼ in.

½ in.

¼ in.

1 To construct the piping, lay the cord along the center of your bias strip, parallel to its long edge (see the sidebar on p. 61 on how to make the bias strip).

2 Fold the fabric in half, aligning the raw edges to enclose the cord. Place the folded bias tape and cord on the sewing-machine bed so that the cord is to the right of the needle.

3 Using a zipper foot and your machine's normal straight-stitch setting (10 to 12 stitches per inch), sew the cord to hold it in place but not too snugly. Leave just enough space—about ¹⁄₁₆ in.—between the cord and your stitching line for the two more rows of stitching you'll be adding in the next steps. Those additional rows will hide this first row of stitching, and your finished edge will look neater. A piping foot and a machine with adjustable needle positions will make this step even easier, since they allow you to feed the corded edge through the groove under the foot and to make small adjustments to your needle position.

4 Next, trim the seam allowance on your piping to ¼ in. This can be done quickly by cutting freehand with a rotary cutter (see the photo at left). Although this method of trimming takes a little practice, it is so much faster than trimming with scissors that it's worth the effort to learn.

5 Clip one end of the piping to neaten it, then from this end pull out enough of the cord so you can clip off ½ in. This empties the end of the piping so you won't be stitching over the cord when you apply the piping (see the illustration at left).

APPLYING THE CORDED PIPING

Before attaching the piping, you need to decide if you want the triangle-shaped facing to be part of the design on the face

The cord starts here.

Offset ⅛ in.

As you approach the clipped piping to turn the corner, use an awl to keep the narrow seam allowances aligned and in place. *(Photo by Grey Crawford.)*

of your collage or to be applied to the back. If the facing is to show on the front, you'll begin by applying the piping to the back side of the collage. If the facing is to be on the back side of the collage in the traditional manner, you'll apply the piping and facing to the front side first, then sew the facing down when it's flipped to the reverse side. By doing this, you'll end up with your bobbin thread making a textured triangle-shaped design on the front.

You'll be aligning the raw edges of the piping so that they are ⅛ in. in from the raw edge of your collage instead of the usual manner of matching raw edges. This offset alignment eliminates the need to grade the seam (which means to stagger-trim seam allowances to eliminate bulk) after the piping is stitched in place. As a renegade sewer, I do whatever it takes to save time and energy without compromising quality.

1 Choose a place to begin applying the piping that won't be too conspicuous, such as the bottom center of the collage.

2 Next, insert the machine needle through the collage ¼ in. from its raw edge, then place the piping so that its empty end is angled toward the seam allowance.

3 Start your first few stitches at the folded edge of the piping, and cross the empty casing to your original line of stitching (see the illustration above).

4 Then stitch just inside the original stitching line one thread closer to the cord, taking care not to stretch the piping's bias edges or the collage underneath. Stitch to within 2 in. of the first corner, and stop in place with the needle down.

5 Hold the piping in place to determine the point where you will turn the corner. At that spot, clip up to but not through your original line of stitching, which should be ¼ in. from the raw edge closest to you. This clip will enable you to pull the piping

Use an awl to push a tiny bit of the piping away from you toward the corner just turned. This provides the ease necessary for the piping to lie flat when it is finally in place between the collage and the facing. *(Photo by Grey Crawford.)*

ENDING THE PIPING

Original stitching line forming piping

The cord ends here.

Stitching line attaching piping to collage

into its new alignment with the second edge as you turn the corner with your needle in the down position.

6 Using an awl or a T-pin, ease a bit of the cord back toward the corner you've just sewn (see the photo above). This extra cord eased inside the piping will be just enough to give you a smooth corner that lies flat when the facing is turned to the opposite side and the cording becomes the outside curve.

7 Continue stitching, clipping at each corner and remembering to ease the cord, until you come back to your starting point. Cut away the excess length of piping, leaving ½ in. for overlap. Again, push back the casing to allow you to cut off the last ½ in. of the cord inside.

By the Way

For a quick finish, don't trim the piping's seam allowances. Instead, with the right side facing you, align the untrimmed raw edges of the piping with the raw edges of the collage and stitch in place. Then turn the seam allowances to the inside of the collage, and stitch along their raw edges, using a zigzag or other decorative stitch to hold them in place. The stitched seam allowances of the piping become a decorative band around the inside edges of the collage, and the bobbin thread is seen as a decorative stitch on the right side of the collage.

8 Finally, overlap the two ends of piping and stitch in place (see the illustration on the facing page).

MAKING THE TRIANGLE-SHAPED FACINGS

Triangle-shaped facings are a snap to make. Traditional quilters will recognize that the triangles used in this technique are "half-square triangles."

1 Begin by cutting 2-in. squares out of fabric that complements your collage. You don't need to use the same fabric for all of the squares. To calculate the number of squares you'll need, divide the distance in inches around your collage by two. Then cut the squares diagonally into triangles.

Cutting out 160 or more triangles is easy to do with just one of your quarter-yard pieces of fabric. With your rotary cutter, cut two 2-in. strips the width of your fabric. Stack these two strips, and cut them into 2-in. squares. Leave the squares stacked, then cut them in half diagonally into triangles (see the top photo at right).

2 Create a chain of triangles by overlapping each long side to the center of the last one and stitching them together ¼ in. from the long edge. It's not crucial that each triangle overlaps the previous one by exactly the same amount because the overall effect of this finishing technique is casual. The chain you've made will be used like a traditional facing.

3 Next, lay the triangle chain on the sewing-machine bed right side up with its long, straight side to the right of the needle. You'll be attaching the facing to the piping by stitching it from the side of the collage opposite the side to which you stitched the piping.

4 Position the collage so the side with the piping is against the facing. This allows you to see where you stitched the piping in

Make a triangle-shaped facing by rotary-cutting strips of fabric that are 2 in. wide by the width of the fabric. Cut 2-in. squares from these strips, then cut the squares in half diagonally. (Photo by Grey Crawford.)

Place the piped collage face down over the right side of the triangle chain so you can see the stitching line that attached the piping. Using that line of stitching as a guide to attach the triangle facing, stitch one thread inside of the original stitching line closer to the piping. (Photo by Grey Crawford.)

An awl is used to form a little valley, allowing the needle to stitch very close to the cord. *(Photo by Grey Crawford.)*

This detail of the inside finish of a vest's shoulder seam shows two ways to use free-motion stitching to attach the triangle facing: zigzag stitches along the edges of the triangle and crisscrossed paths of forward and reverse stitching. *(Photo by Jack Deutsch.)*

the first step (see the bottom photo on p. 65). These stitches are your guide for attaching the facing to the collage.

5 Next, sew another line of stitching, again trying to stitch just one thread's breadth closer to the piping so that the previous rows of stitching won't show when the facing is flipped to the other side and stitched down. To help me sew closer to the piping, before I start stitching I run a blunt tool along the seam next to the cording to form a little valley to stitch in (see the photo above left).

6 Clip the facing to the stitching at the corners, just as you did when applying the piping.

7 After the facing is stitched in place, trim the corners of your collage diagonally, being careful not to clip through the stitching.

8 Next, fold the triangles over to the reverse side of your collage, enclosing the seam allowances.

9 Making sure the triangles lay flat and taut, stitch them down. You can either free-motion zigzag close to the triangle edges or use free-motion sewing to make crisscrossed paths by stitching forward and in reverse (see the photo above right). I use both techniques, spontaneously switching between the two.

Final Laundering

Your facings must pucker to match the texture of the rest of your collage. So as you did before, run your collage through the washer and dryer. If it is a small piece, you can liberally spray all the newly added pieces of fabric with water and put the collage directly into the dryer with a towel for a buffer.

When the collage comes out of the dryer, settle down with a good movie or a compelling audio book, and trim off the dangling thread ends and excess frayed edges. Duck-billed embroidery scissors are my favorite tool for this task. Just be careful not to trim the frayed edges too close to the stitching. The edges need to be evenly trimmed on similar fabrics so that the fraying looks intentional, but not all of the fabrics will sport frayed edges of the same length.

Creativity Begets Creativity

One of my life's enduring treasures is the inspiration I get from those attending my classes. I hesitate to use the word students because I'm often learning more than I teach from the many talented people I work with. Linda Anderson is one of those people who learned the art of fabric collage and ran with it. She's developed a beautiful lacy edge that she calls the "free-motion edge." It's grown from her experiments with fabric collage and thinking about the edge as a continuation of the quilt instead of as an enclosing edge added like a frame.

Linda has developed this free-motion edge into a "doodle edge," where the free-motion stitching extends beyond the edge

PREPARING TO SEW A FREE-MOTION EDGE

Center a 6-in.-wide strip of heavyweight stabilizer beneath the outer edge of your collage.

6 in.

Collage

Water-soluble stabilizer

of the quilt. The first steps in designing and stitching her collages are the same ones I've described, but instead of ending the free-motion stitching where the quilt ends, she doodles the stitching onto a stabilizer, creating leaves, swirls, and abstract shapes that echo the designs of her collage (see the bottom illustration on the facing page).

1 After laundering and squaring your collage as described on pp. 57-59, remove ⅛ in. to ¼ in. of the batting or muslin from the edges that will have free-motion edging, leaving only the two layers of fabric from the collage and the backing.

2 Cut a strip of heavy water-soluble stabilizer such as Super Solvy that's 6 in. wide and the length of the edge to be stitched. (If you're working on a large collage, work on one piece of stabilizer at a time and overlap additional pieces as

needed.) If you don't have access to heavy stabilizer, see p. 165 for instructions on bonding three layers of lightweight stabilizer.

3 Next, prepare your machine for free-motion stitching, and center the quilt's raw edge over the strip of stabilizer (see the illustration on the facing page). You will be stitching the edge in two stages.

4 For the first stage, stitch in all directions and concentrate on the raw edge of the quilt, making sure the edge is covered with thread. This can be done with a straight stitch, zigzag stitch, or any combination of stitches.

5 The second time you stitch the edge, feather the stitching in toward the body of the quilt where it gradually ends, blending in with the previous stitching on the collage (see the top illustration at right). The more stitching you do at the edge of the quilt, the better it will retain its shape.

6 Trim the excess stabilizer from the stitched edge.

7 To dissolve the stabilizer, simply dip the stitched edge in tepid water instead of immersing the whole collage.

8 Finally, lay the collage flat to dry, or use a hair dryer to speed up the process. If you're really impatient, Linda says the whole thing can go in the dryer, but you may need to iron the edge flat if it's distorted.

Now that you've mastered the basic steps in making a collage, you're no doubt ready to fly with the technique and to use it for other projects. The next chapter will show how I've been using collage to make vests that are timeless accessories for anyone's wardrobe.

SEWING A FREE-MOTION EDGE

1. Concentrate squiggly stitches or zigzag stitches close to the raw edge.

2. Embellish the edge, blending stitches into the stitching on the body of the collage.

CREATING A DOODLE EDGE

Extend free-motion stitching onto a stabilizer to create lacy shapes that echo the motifs along the edge of the collage.

5

Collaging
a Vest

Vests are mainstay wardrobe accessories and look sensational when embellished with collage. In this chapter, I'll give some suggestions to help you design a stunning reversible collaged vest. Next, you'll learn to adapt a vest pattern that you can use over and over again as a blank canvas for collage and for a variety of other wearable art techniques. And you'll learn my techniques for fine-tuning the fit of that pattern to your body.

Designing a Vest Collage

If you're making this vest for your first collage, review chapter 1 before you begin your design. Instructions on how to create fabric collage and suggestions for inspiration and design are covered in detail.

There's a knack to keeping the wearable in wearable art. Although you are working on one large, flat surface, you will actually be creating two compositions: one composition is on the back of the vest and the other is on the two fronts. I consider the back of my vest to be the canvas for my primary composition—the one where most of the action takes place and the story is told.

The two fronts work together as one composition, which is the composition that people see when they're having a conversation with the wearer. Although the fronts relate to the back and work as part of the whole design, I like to keep their composition subtler. No matter how spectacular your garment is, you should be wearing it and not vice versa.

The composition on the back of your vest establishes the theme and tells your story. You'll recall that you start your collage by cutting out motifs (with an ⅛-in. margin) that support your theme. When you have a selection of cut-out motifs to work with, arrange them on the back of the muslin underlining first, paying particular

(Photo opposite by Grey Crawford; photo above by Jack Deutsch.)

"Imagine Meeting You Here": This vest sports its major motifs on the back, where most of its story is told. *(Photo by Jack Deutsch.)*

"Muses Do Their Thing": A bridge of fabric motifs and knotted ribbon connects the composition on the back of this vest with the design elements on the front. *(Photo by Jack Deutsch.)*

attention to creating a focal point that is in an interesting location (see pp. 14–16).

Next, use more motifs to act as stepping stones that will move the eye from the back to the fronts of the vest. These motifs are placed under the arms where they're not likely to be seen very often. Because they aren't star players, keep them more subdued.

Once you've created a bridge from the back composition to the fronts, add motifs to establish your theme on the front of the vest. For now, you'll need to imagine what your vest will look like when the right side of it overlaps the left. If you've chosen a style without an overlap, picture the two fronts as they'll appear side-by-side when they're being worn. You won't have a chance to really see what they look like until all of your collage fabrics are pinned in place, so you'll have to see them in your mind's eye as you design.

"Putting fried eggs on your chest" is one of the most common mistakes that someone can make when designing wearables, but fortunately it's also an easy one to avoid. When looking for a place to put cabbage-rose motifs, for instance, group them high on one shoulder like a corsage, rather than placing a balanced pair lower on both sides of the chest. Or you can let them land near the overlapping points at the front or at the lower edges of the garment. Just be sure you don't create bull's eyes where you don't want them!

Dramatic effects can be created when you consider how the front of your vest will look when the two sides overlap. For example, a motif featured at the point of closure on the right front will have greater impact if it is outlined against a contrasting fabric on the left. When motifs on both fronts meet in an interesting way, it creates an effect that makes sense to the viewer. This happens, for instance, when a flower on one side of the vest nestles into an arrangement of leaves on the other, or when a fish on one side swims toward a wave on the other. A little forethought can go a long way toward designing vest fronts that work together.

If you have motifs that would look strange if they were partly lopped off, keep them at least 1½ in. away from the outer edges of the underlining. Since you don't know how much the collage will shrink, it's impossible to know how much of the outer edges may need to be trimmed when the collaged vest is cut to your exact pattern. Planning for the possibility that you'll cut off 1 in. at the edges will make it less likely that you'll lose parts of your major motifs after the vest has been laundered.

"Hawaiian Springtime": Careful placement of motifs helps the two fronts work together as one composition. *(Photo by Jack Deutsch.)*

The closure on this vest makes a dramatic statement because the angel on the right front of the garment is emphasized by the fabric motifs on the left. *(Photo by Jack Deutsch.)*

Check your layout to be sure that major motifs are kept at least 1 in. from the edges so they won't be trimmed off later. Here, the large flowers along the bottom edge will be incorporated into shaped edges. *(Photo by Grey Crawford.)*

Modifying a Vest Pattern for Collage

Making a three-dimensional garment from a one-piece, two-dimensional pattern may sound impossible. But if you eliminate the side seams from a vest of simple design, you'll have a one-piece pattern that has only shoulder seams. The design will flow from the back of the garment to the front without being interrupted by side-seam lines. If you have a favorite two-piece vest pattern without darts or other design-line seams, it can be easily modified to create a single-piece pattern that is appropriate for collage.

1 To begin modifying a pattern, overlap the vest front and back pattern pieces at the side seams, matching the seamlines, then pin the two pieces together along the seamline (see the illustration at left). Trace this one-piece pattern onto another paper if you plan to use your original pattern again.

2 Remove the entire shoulder-seam allowance so that the front and back shoulders can be butted together when the vest is finally assembled. Also cut off all remaining seam allowances, including those at the neckline, front, bottom, and armscye.

If you are using a pattern of your own and have adapted it as described above, you may want to skip to the section on "Fitting the Vest Pattern" on p. 76 now. If you wish to use the patterns used for the Sewjourner's vests shown in this book, read on (see Resources on p. 168).

MODIFYING THE VEST PATTERN

Place on fold.

Back   Front

Seamlines

Overlap the pattern front and back, matching the side seams. Trim away all other seam allowances.

Pattern-Making Materials

To make a pattern for fitting, I prefer to trace patterns on Mönster paper imported from Sweden. It's similar to nonwoven interfacing but drapes like muslin and can be sewn with a basting stitch. This makes it possible to use your pattern for fitting without having to make a separate muslin shell. However, use whatever is easiest for you to obtain. You are likely to find pattern tracing paper, with or without grids, at most fabric stores and in sewing-notions catalogs.

My students have used a variety of materials to make their patterns: sew-in interfacing, tissue paper, examining-table paper from a medical-supply outlet, rolls of paper table covering purchased at a party-supply store, and newsprint-roll ends sold for a few dollars at a newspaper office. Once you have a pattern that fits, make a sturdy copy from tag board, or reinforce a paper pattern with iron-on craft bonding material such as Craft Bond. Be sure to use a Teflon pressing sheet over the Craft Bond to avoid getting the adhesive on your iron.

SEWJOURNER'S PATTERNS

The patterns for my collaged vests have no side seams and are specially designed to flatter a mature figure as well as those of our more petite sisters. They are cut high at the lower center back, just 2 in. to 3 in. below the waist. This surprises women who are used to pulling their tops down to cover their fannies. I'm fully aware of *my* mature figure, so when I designed my first pattern for collage, I wanted a vest that was flattering without being matronly.

Most vests, if they aren't designed to stop near the waist, stop in a horizontal line 6 in. to 10 in. below the waist. That's exactly the area where the hips are the largest. Unless the vest is the same color as the garments underneath, that straight line just emphasizes the hip width. I've also observed that longer vests, because they fit closer to the body than a jacket, tend to ride up and sit on a large derriere, which draws attention to what we hope will be overlooked.

Contrary to what you might think, this short vest back is more flattering, especially when worn over a dress or a long top with matching pants or skirt. Viewed from behind, the bottom lines of the vest move diagonally upward from the sides. The observer's eye is drawn to the narrower area close to the wearer's waist, which visually diminishes the hips. In front, the illusion of a longer torso is created by the downward diagonal lines from the hips to the front points ending at the center of each thigh, emphasizing the length of the body rather than its girth.

If you're using my Sewjourner's pattern designs, they are ready to use for collage as noted in their instructions.

Identifying Your Size

The instructions in this section, which apply specifically to Sewjourner's patterns, will help you choose the pattern size you should work with. Before you select a size,

"Touched by an Angel."
(Photo by Jack Deutsch.)

decide whether you prefer a vest that fits loosely, close to the body, or somewhere in between. While I'm not an advocate of one-size-fits-all, experience tells me that a single size in my vest designs can accommodate many body types with a range of bust sizes, depending on how the wearer likes them to fit. Notice I said accommodate, which doesn't mean fit, but we'll perfect the fit later in the chapter.

The chart on p. 76 is a guide to help you choose the size that will fit the way you want it to. Keep in mind that my patterns are designed with generous ease to allow several layers of clothing or loose-fitting tops to be worn under them, so you can take that into account as you choose your best size. For instance, if you have a 36-in. bust and like a slightly fitted look, start by choosing a size M pattern. Although M is indicated for a 35-in. bust, it will undoubtedly provide sufficient ease to fit close to your body and fit over a cotton blouse or a knit T-shirt.

However, if you never leave home with less than two layers of clothing under your vests, or if you're inclined to slip on a vest over a heavy sweater or a loose-fitting dress, a size L will probably be your best size. Choose the size that comes closest to your body size and your preferred style of fit.

Fitting the Vest Pattern

There are fitting criteria that you must pay attention to in order to develop a pattern for a vest that looks good on your unique frame. I've got a fitting method that will,

with a minimum of fuss, provide you with a pattern for a garment that fits you really well.

The fitting techniques I'll describe in the following sections are the ones that have worked for me and have helped others create vest patterns that they use over and over. But by all means, if you have another method that works for you and that you understand, use it. Just be sure that you use some method to fit your pattern before you invest the time and creative energy necessary to make a collaged vest.

Whether you use a commercial pattern that you're familiar with or one of the Sewjourner's patterns, you'll begin by fitting the paper pattern of the vest to your body. If you are using my pattern, trace the half-pattern of your size and cut it out. Then label the pattern—for example, "Sewjourner's Vest, Size L"—to help you remember which one you're working with. As you work, make fitting notes on your paper pattern so that you'll have a record to

SEWJOURNER'S PATTERN SIZES

Pattern size	S	M	L	XL	XXL	XXXL	XXXXL	XXXXXL
Bust size	32	35	38	41	44	47	50	53

refer to when you make a muslin shell to check the fit.

You'll benefit from having a sewing partner help you make adjustments. To prepare for your fitting, don't strip down to your scanties; instead, put on the bulkiest garment you'll be likely to wear under your vest. If a vest has been carefully fitted, a comfortably loose one that looks good over a turtleneck with oversized set-in sleeves will become stylishly baggy when the vest is worn over a knit T-shirt, yet it will still hang right on your body.

1 To begin fitting, butt the pattern's shoulder seams and hold them together with removable tape. Slip into the paper half-pattern, having your partner pin its center back foldline to the garment you're wearing so that it lines up with the center of your spine.

2 Check the general fit of the vest. The center back should lay along your spine without creating vertical bulges or pulling the sides out of alignment. The back neckline should lay smoothly about ½ in. below the bone that protrudes at the base of your neck. Cutting the vest neckline slightly lower than a jewel neckline will accommodate collars on garments worn under the vest.

The front opening edges should lay flat across your chest, and there should be ample overlap where the vest fastens. The points at the lower edge should line up with the centers of your thighs.

Pay particular attention to the armscyes, which are often neglected in fitting a vest. They should lay smoothly against your body at both the front and the back of the arm. There should be plenty of room for a sleeve to fit through the armscye without bunching up.

If you're lucky, the paper pattern fits you perfectly, and you're ready to cut out your muslin underlining and start on your col-

lage. In that case, turn to p. 83 and let the fun begin. On the other hand, you may need to make and try on more than one pattern to determine which size gives the best fit across your chest and around your bust. More than likely, you may simply need to fine-tune the fit of this size.

FITTING THE DETAILS

If your paper pattern doesn't fit exactly, you may have to adjust the back, neck, shoulders, and armscye. You should also check the length of the back as well as the location of the bottom points of the front.

1 While you're still wearing your paper pattern, have your partner check the fit across the back. Here's where a fitting partner will be a necessity. If the back is just a little too tight, you can add up to ½ in. at the back foldline, giving you an extra 1 in. across the back of the garment. Or if you have a narrow back, you can cut up to ½ in. off at the back foldline.

Then make any adjustments necessary to restore the original outline of the back neckline. On most garments, making an alteration on the back would require that a similar increase or decrease be made to the front. However, because there's a generous overlap at the front closure of Sewjourner's patterns, it's unnecessary to make changes to the front after making slight alterations to the back pattern pieces.

2 If your neck is small, remove the gap that's created on the back neckline. If it's just a tiny gap, don't worry—your three

By the Way

Goody hair tape, the pink tape with the pinked edge used to tame "spit curls" in the good old days, works great for making pattern alterations. It stays in place but can be easily repositioned. You'll find it in the hair accessories section of your drug store.

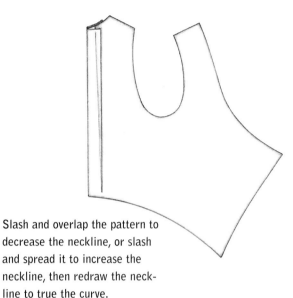

Slash and overlap the pattern to decrease the neckline, or slash and spread it to increase the neckline, then redraw the neckline to true the curve.

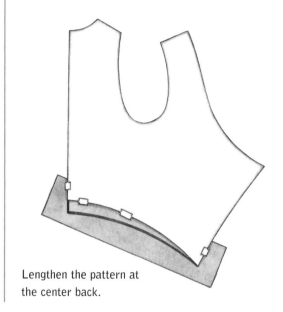

Lengthen the pattern at the center back.

layers of puckered fabric will make it disappear. If it's a large gap, slash from the center of the bulge to but not through the bottom cutting line, leaving a ⅛-in. margin there (see the above left illustration). Overlap until the gap disappears, tape the pattern in place, then redraw the neckline curve.

3 If your neck is large, you may need to enlarge the neckline. That's easily done by slightly trimming the neckline at the cutting line. Keep in mind that the amount you trim away from the pattern neckline will be doubled in the finished garment. In

other words, ¼ in. trimmed from the pattern will increase the neckline by ½ in.

4 Next, check the length of the back. The back cutting line of the pattern is designed to extend 2 in. below your waistline. It's easiest to shorten or lengthen the vest by redrawing the bottom edge. Determine how much shorter (or longer) you want the vest to be at the center back, then redraw the curve between the center back and the point at the lower front.

If you're adding length, you'll need to tape on more paper at the bottom of the pattern (see the above right illustration). When you add length in the hope that it will cover a protruding derriere, don't add so much that the back of the vest must curve outward to accommodate the fanny. The bottom edge should just comfortably skim that area as the vest falls in a straight line from the shoulders.

5 Now check the placement of the shoulder seams. The design of this vest allows for a small shoulder pad on an average-size person. The edges closest to the

Check to be sure your vest falls in a straight line from your shoulders to 2 in. to 3 in. below your waist. *(Photo by Grey Crawford.)*

arm on the shoulder seam may need to be shortened for someone with sloping shoulders or for someone who never wears shoulder pads. Then check that the seamline lies at the crest of the shoulder. If necessary, redraw the seamline, making sure it is neither too far forward nor too far back.

6 Check the shoulder width. Someone with broad shoulders might want to add a bit of width at the armscye edge of the shoulder seam so that the upper part of the vest doesn't seem too skimpy. Simply as a design element, you can extend the shoulderline to broaden the shoulders. This change looks like a little capped sleeve (see the photo at right).

To widen the shoulder, extend the shoulder's cutting line 1½ in. to 2 in., then draw a 2-in. line at a 90-degree angle down from the shoulderline and taper it back to the midpoint of the original cutting line of the armscye.

7 If the front is slightly skimpy over your bust, move the cutting line out as much as ¾ in. past the original cutting line. To do this, tape a piece of pattern paper to the front of your pattern. Starting 2 in. below the shoulder seam, draw a line that tapers out to add the desired fullness. You may need to move the front overlap point as well so that you maintain a smooth line from your shoulder to that point. The vest fronts should overlap enough to give a comfortable fit without pulling.

Sewjourner's patterns have enough overlap that an adjustment of 2 in. to 3 in. can be made in the girth without distorting the design. If the vest front is too wide across the chest, you can shave up to ¾ in. off the front cutting line (see the illustration below). Again, check the placement of the front overlap point after making this alteration.

FITTING THE FRONT

— · — · — Narrower
- - - - - Wider

When altering the width of the vest front, note that the points at the lower front remain at the same length.

Extend the shoulder's back and front cutting lines equally 1½ in. to 2 in. into the armscye, and draw a new cutting line that meets the original one to create a shoulder cap. *(Photo by Grey Crawford.)*

Change the location of the lower point to keep it at the center of the thigh.

Shorten and relocate the point at the front of the thigh.

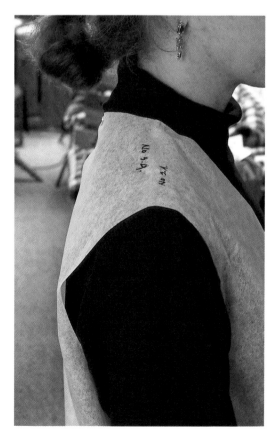

Buckles at the front or back of the armscye indicate that an alteration must be made to the pattern to achieve perfect fit. *(Photo by Grey Crawford.)*

8 Finally, check the location of the points at the bottom front of the vest. They're most flattering when they point to the middle of the thighs. If you're short, you may wish to raise them 1 in. to 2 in. To relocate the point, tape a piece of paper to the bottom of your pattern. Mark the new position of the point, then taper the cutting lines back to the original cutting lines (see the illustration above).

FITTING THE ARMSCYE

As I've become familiar with the way vests fit a variety of body shapes and sizes, I've noticed that the fit of the armscye in particular is a dead giveaway as to whether care has been given to fitting the garment. The problem is especially noticeable on a full-busted figure. So let's take care of any gapping armholes.

It's helpful to understand why an armscye gaps in the first place. It's because we're taking a flat piece of fabric and asking it to fit a shape that is far from flat. That's why darts, pleats, and folds were invented. In the design of this vest, however, we're depending on the suppleness of the fabric to accommodate the curved planes of our body.

On a full-busted figure, there's typically not enough suppleness in the fabric to allow the armscye to lay flat, so a gap appears and we're tempted to put a dart there to remove the excess fabric. The same thing happens when a flat piece of fabric lays over a rounded back: A buckle appears at the back of the armscye (see the photo on the facing page). On another project, a dart would be fine, but we need to keep the construction of this vest dart-free so we can lay out a collage on its flat surface.

You may have a slight gap at either side of the armscye or on the front edge of the pattern. By slight, I mean that you notice it, but you can hardly pinch up the pattern to remove the excess fullness. There's no more than 1/2 in. too much fullness. You can choose to take in that gap now as you prepare your master pattern, or you can take care of it by making an easy adjustment to the vest itself by easing in the fullness when you're finishing it. You might want to read p. 90 to find out how to take in the gap when finishing so that you can decide now whether or not to make a change in the paper pattern. Here's how to alter the pattern to get rid of a larger gap at either the front or the back of the armscye.

1 Pinch the gap closed, forming a little tuck, and place a mark at the crease of this temporary tuck. Also place marks at either side of the tuck where it begins (see the photo above).

2 Slash the pattern through the center of the gap from the armhole edge, where you placed the first mark, to within 1/8 in. of the center back or the front neckline. Then overlap the pattern, matching the two outside marks, and tape the overlap in place (see the illustration at right). Making this while keeping the pattern flat.

Pins mark the spots on either side of a tuck that's pinched up to remove excess fullness. *(Photo by Grey Crawford.)*

ALTERING THE ARMSCYE

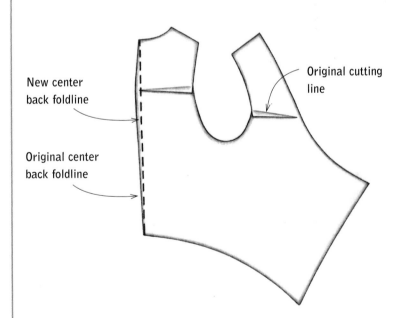

New center back foldline

Original cutting line

Original center back foldline

Cut and slash the pattern to eliminate gaps at the front and back armscye.

CORRECTING A GAP AT THE VEST FRONT

Slash the pattern toward the edge where the excess fullness points.

ALTERING THE SIZE OF THE ARMSCYE

Raise or lower the depth of the armscye.

3 Because the center back line will no longer be straight after altering the back armscye, redraw the cutting lines to return them to their original shape. To true the center back line, position a straightedge from the uppermost point to the lowermost point, and draw a straight line joining them. To correct irregular lines around the armscye, use a french curve or a flexible ruler to draw a smooth line.

4 If there is a buckle above the overlap on the front edge of your pattern, pinch up the gap and pin to mark it as described in step 1. When you pinch up the gap, notice the angle that's created by the excess fabric. It will point toward the front of the armscye or toward the bottom edge of the vest. When you slash the pattern, angle your cut toward that point (see the top illustration at left). Overlap and tape the pattern, then true the cutting line.

5 Next, consider the size of the armscye. If it's too deep to fit the garments you'll be wearing under your vest, tape some pattern paper to the pattern at the lower curve of the armhole. Mark the amount you want to raise the armscye, then redraw the curve to the middle of the armscye at both the front and the back of the pattern.

6 To accommodate deeper sleeves, mark the desired depth and redraw the cutting line, tapering to the middle of the armscye (see the bottom illustration at left). You may want to raise the armscye when you make a vest to wear over tank tops in the summer.

By the Way

It's a cinch to alter curved lines when you use an architect's flexible ruler. Just mold it into the desired curve, then draw against that ruler to create a smooth line in the position you want.

Now that you've altered your basic pattern to fit you perfectly, you might want to make some changes in the shape of the vest to suit your personal style. Think of this pattern—and every pattern—as being similar to a chili recipe: All cooks may use the same basic ingredients, but each one adds a little of this or that to make the dish her own.

There are many design possibilities, as shown in the illustration at right. You can round the front overlapping points or the bottom points for a softer look. Or you can cut off both of the overlap margins on the front to create an entirely new look with a vest that will always be worn open. The vertical line that this alteration creates gives a very slimming effect. As you make your vest, you'll probably think of other possibilities. Make a note of them to try in the future.

Making a Clean Copy of the Pattern

Once you've finished altering your paper pattern, make a clean copy of it without slashes or taped-on edges. Then transfer all of the text from the original pattern onto your permanent pattern before you continue. This will remind you of the details of using the pattern when you bring it out for future projects.

Making a Muslin Shell

Once you're satisfied that the altered pattern fits satisfactorily, you can use it to make a muslin shell. This isn't an essential step, especially if you haven't had to make alterations or if your alterations have been minor. On the other hand, this will give you a better idea of how any alterations you have made will look in fabric. It's a crucial step if your body is not symmetrical, since you may need to make a separate

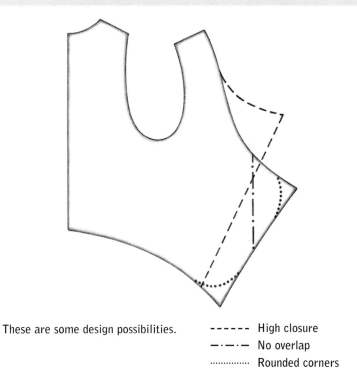

These are some design possibilities.

- - - - - - High closure
— · — · — No overlap
············· Rounded corners

set of alterations for the second half of your pattern.

1 Begin by laying out your altered pattern with the center back on the fold and cutting it out exactly on the cutting lines except for the shoulders. You'll need 2 yd. of muslin folded in half on the crosswise grain.

2 For ease in trying on your fitting shell, add ½-in. seam allowances at the shoulders.

3 Next, sew the shell together at the shoulders. Try on your muslin shell, keeping in mind that it will have much less body than the finished collaged fabric. It probably fits you perfectly, but there's still an opportunity to make changes if they're necessary and to adjust your master pattern accordingly.

YARDAGE REQUIREMENTS FOR MUSLIN UNDERLINING

Fabric width	45 in.	52 in.–54 in.	60 in.
Size XS–S:	1½ yd.	¾ yd.	¾ yd.
Size M–XL:	1¾ yd.	1¾ yd.	⅞ yd.
Size XXL–XXXXXL:	2 yd.	2 yd.	2 yd.

CUTTING THE UNDERLINING

Selvage

½ in.

Place pattern ½ in. from fold.

Pattern

Cutting line

1 in.

Selvage

Cutting Out the Muslin Underlining

Your vest will be layered the same as the sample collage described in chapter 1, having a lining, a muslin underlining, and a collaged surface. Your underlining is the middle layer in the fabric sandwich, the layer on which the collage will be sewn. For the underlining, use either high-quality 100% cotton muslin or, for a warmer vest, cotton flannel. Check the chart at left to find out how much muslin to buy. A good-quality muslin doesn't need prewashing, but flannel needs to be washed several times because it tends to shrink so much.

1 Start by ironing any creases out of the muslin, then fold it in half on the cross-grain and lay it on your cutting mat.

2 Place the center back of your pattern ½ in. from the fabric fold. This extra measure allows for shrinkage across the back of your vest in the laundering stage.

3 As you cut out your underlining, leave a 1-in. margin between the cutting line marked on your pattern and the line you actually cut on (see the illustration at left). This margin will provide for shrinkage in all directions. It's not essential that you cut this margin with precision. The amount your vest will shrink is unpredictable, so it doesn't matter if the margin is more than 1 in., but make sure it isn't less. Now put your master pattern aside, since you won't be using it for a while.

Cutting Out the Lining

Since I'm never sure how my vest design will develop when I start, I usually haven't made a decision at this point about which lining fabric to use. So I design the collage on the muslin underlining alone and choose a lining after the layout is finished. If you also plan to wait, skip to the next section.

On the other hand, you may have a fully imagined concept of your finished vest and have the perfect lining fabric for your reversible garment. In that case, you have the option of pinning and sewing the collage on the muslin underlining and the lining at the same time, rather than working on just the underlining first.

1 Begin by spreading the yardage for your lining on your cutting table wrong side up.

2 Lay out the muslin underlining on top of the lining, then using your underlining as a pattern, cut out the lining. From now on treat the two layers as a single piece of fabric.

Collaging the Vest

Fiber artists, your canvas lies before you! Proceed in the spirit of play, and enjoy the creative process designing your vest.

1 Spread out your cut-to-the-pattern muslin underlining (or stacked lining and underlining with the muslin on top) on your worktable. If you're working on an asymmetric pattern, make sure that the right front of the underlining lies to your right. This is not a concern when you design with a symmetrical vest pattern since both sides are cut the same.

"September Song": The outer edges of leaves create an undulating shaped edge at the lower back of this vest. *(Photo by Jack Deutsch.)*

2 Following the design suggestions beginning on p. 15, arrange your major theme motifs.

3 If you've decided to include shaped edges on your vest, lay out your fabrics in a way that will create these lovely undulating edges. Look for large motif shapes with outlines that are interesting but not too sharply pointed or exaggerated.

By the Way

An Olfa rotary cutter with a measuring arm will help you make quick work of cutting out your muslin underlining with a margin.

The outermost edges of each motif must lie on the muslin, which will help stabilize the finished edge. *(Photo by Grey Crawford.)*

Shaped edges blend into piped and faced edges to create variety. *(Photo by Jack Deutsch.)*

Arrange your motifs along the hemline or at the front edge of the vest on the muslin underlining. Since shrinkage typically takes up most of the extra 1 in. I allowed when I cut out my underlining, I place the motifs at the very edge of the muslin. However, be careful that the entire motif is backed by the muslin. The outer edges of the motifs should create a gently curving line with no part of the motif dipping below the muslin backing.

The less complicated the outline of the edge on the face of the collage, the easier it will be to match that edge with different but similarly shaped motifs on the lining side (see "Lining a Shaped Edge" on p. 120).

FILLING IN THE DESIGN

When you're satisfied with the layout of your theme motifs, it's time to fill in the empty spaces using your background fabrics.

1 Following the directions on pp. 16–19, select and cut your background fabrics. You'll be slipping them under the edges of your motif fabrics. Remember to use pieces that are at least as large as your palm, and overlap all edges by ½ in.

By the Way

If the outer edge of your shaped motif is deeply incised, its exaggerated points will twist and turn after they've been finished with satin stitching and laundered. This can be a wonderful effect—if you've planned for it or if you are willing to live with it. To make a test sample, follow the directions for finishing shaped edges on pp. 92-93, then launder the sample to see what effect you're likely to get from these satin-stiched cuts on your vest border.

This sample shows a deeply incised shaped edge finished with free-motion satin stitching. Note its three-dimensional quality compared with the flatter edge achieved with shallower curves shown in the photo on p. 93. *(Photo by Grey Crawford.)*

Position background fabrics behind motifs, then layer the motif fabrics to give the impression of depth. *(Photo by Grey Crawford.)*

When the collaged fabrics are pinned in place, check the effect of overlapping the fronts as they will appear when being worn. The two fronts work together to create one composition. *(Photo by Grey Crawford.)*

2 Pin all of your collage elements securely in place. You must be able to pick up the vest from any side and move it around without any pieces falling off and without any edges flapping loose. It's not worth skimping on this step: Doing a thorough job of pinning now will diminish your frustration later when you start doing free-motion sewing.

3 Now check how your design looks when the two fronts meet. Place your vest collage-side down on your worktable, and bring the two sides forward to overlap or meet in the front as they will when the vest is worn. Step back, view your overall design, and make any last adjustments to it before you begin sewing.

Take care to cover the collaged garment consistently with a moderate amount of free-motion stitching. *(Photo by Jack Deutsch.)*

Making the Lining

Linings can be as simple or as complex as you want them to be. If this is your first collaged vest, I suggest that you line it with a single fabric that relates to the theme and the colors of the collage. If you'd like to design a lining that has lots of character, you'll find suggestions in chapter 7.

Since your vest will be reversible, choose a lining fabric that you'd like to be seen in. You may not think that you'll ever want to wear you vest lining side out, but the lining will be surprisingly transformed when you do free-motion stitching. The threads in your bobbin, especially if they contrast with your lining or if they sparkle, will give the lining a beautifully textured surface that you'll want to show off.

If you were waiting to finish your collage before selecting your lining, you can use the chart on p. 84 to determine how much fabric you'll need.

1 To make your lining, use your collaged vest, with the pins in place, as a pattern. With the lining fabric wrong side up on your worktable, place the collage with its wrong side against the lining fabric, making

sure both are lying as flat as possible. If your lining fabric's design is one-directional, take care that the top of the design is placed at the top of your vest.

2 Pin the collage to the lining around the edges to hold it in place. Add a few more pins to the middle of your collage, too, then cut out the lining to match the vest exactly.

Free-Motion Stitching on a Garment

When stitching on a garment, there are a few things to keep in mind that you wouldn't have to consider if you were making a wall hanging.

First, the amount of stitching you do on wearables will affect the hand of the finished garments. If you overstitch a wall hanging, the wall won't care. But if you overstitch your vest, the collage will become as stiff as a board and *you* will care. In areas that are stitched so flat that no fabric puffs up between the rows of stitching, the fabric will remain flat and barely textured even after laundering.

For my collaged garments, I have used many different brands of threads in a wide variety of fibers. My sewing machine has its favorites, and undoubtedly yours will too. I use mostly Sulky, Madiera, YLI, and Kreinik metallic, rayon, and other novelty threads since those are the ones most available to me, but there are other good brands worth trying.

I've read that metallic threads are too weak or too abrasive to use in both the top

By the Way

Some metallic threads are scratchy on bare skin. Since I sometimes wear a vest over a dropped neckline, I no longer use metallics for finishing the edges of the triangle-shaped facings near the neckline.

and the bobbin at the same time. I've also been advised not to use rayon and metallic threads together because the metallic will wear on the weaker rayon threads, causing them to break.

Having shared this information, I must say that it makes sense to me. However, before I'd learned of these potential problems, they hadn't occurred to me, and I'd already stitched many garments with rayon and metallic threads of all kinds used in every imaginable combination. I'm happy to say that those garments are still intact and show no signs of threads breaking down after several years' wear and laundering. Experiment and see what works for you.

Once you've chosen your threads, follow the directions on pp. 50-55 for using free-motion stitching to join the three layers together. After you've finished embellishing your vest, launder it, following the instructions on pp. 57-58.

Using Your Pattern to Cut Out the Laundered Vest

Your vest probably looks a little shaggy after its trip through the laundry, but you'll have to agree it's gaining character and becoming more appealing.

1 Once your vest has been laundered, retrieve your pattern for use in cutting your vest to size. Fold the vest in half to find the center back, then mark it with a pin at the top and at the bottom.

2 Spread your vest open again, and smooth it flat with your hands. Resist any temptation to iron it. If the vest has heat-set lumps and bumps, you can use steam to help flatten it, but don't even think of setting the sole plate of your iron against the collage or it will lose its beautiful texture.

3 Lay your paper pattern on each side of the vest in turn, matching the center back of the pattern to the pins you've used to mark the center back. If you find that one side of the vest has shrunk so much that it is now slightly shorter than the pattern cutting line, don't panic. This rarely happens, but it won't make any significant difference if it does. Remember, these patterns have lots of fitting ease, and ¼ in. one way or the other won't be noticeable.

4 If one side is considerably shorter than your pattern, lay the pattern on this side, and match the center back foldline of the pattern with your two pins marking the vest's center back. Hold it in place with weights or pins, then trim off the ragged edges of the vest using a rotary cutter (my preference) or scissors, following the cutting lines of the pattern. When you come to the short edge, lift your pattern and clean-cut that edge, blending the cut back to the edges that were cut according to the pattern (see the illustration below).

5 Next, fold your vest in half again, and lay it on your cutting board with the

IF THE VEST SHRINKS MORE THAN EXPECTED

Clean-cut the short edge.

Pattern cutting line

Frayed collage edge

"Stalking": The back vent in a vest is purely decorative. It's a vestige of menswear in an age when men wore long vests and coats and carried long swords.
(Photo by Jack Deutsch.)

uncut side down. Use the top side of the vest itself, which is the side that you have already trimmed to shape, as the pattern for cutting out the other half—not the paper pattern.

6 If there's no short side to adjust for, lay the vest out flat and use the paper pattern to cut out each side in turn, matching the center back of the pattern to the center back of the vest. If you intend to have a vent in the back, make the cut about ¼ in. smaller than you want the finished vent to be.

7 Before finishing the edges, always try on the vest. Butt the shoulders, and pin them securely in place. You may still need to make a few adjustments. If the armscyes feel snug, cut them a little deeper. If the front doesn't fall quite right, correct it by adjusting the shoulder seam.

8 Take care of any gaps at the neckline, front-opening edge, or armholes now. Sew a long machine stitch (5mm) through the gapping area, beginning and ending 3 in. on either side, then pull up the bobbin thread to ease in the excess fabric, and knot the thread tails to secure them. It's amazing how much easing—1 in. or more—can be done on collaged fabric without detection. The eased fabric will be held in place when the edging is stitched on.

Camouflaging the Shoulder Seams

When you're satisfied with the vest's fit, you're ready to join the shoulder fronts and backs using a butted seam.

1 Start by cutting two ¾-in. bias strips from fabric that complements your lining fabric. Each should be the length of the shoulder seams.

2 With wrong sides together, align one raw edge of a back shoulder seam with the center of a bias strip (see the illustration

SEWING THE SHOULDER SEAMS

Wrong side of ¾-in. bias strip

Position one back shoulder seam along the centerline of the bias strip with wrong sides together, then stitch in place with a serpentine or zigzag stitch.

Shoulder

on the facing page). Stitch the two together, using a zigzag stitch or serpentine stitch.

3 Next, butt the front shoulder seam against the back, and stitch it to the bias strip, too. Add one more row of zigzag or serpentine stitching down the middle to hold the two raw shoulder seams in place (see the illustration at right). Repeat for the other shoulder.

4 Finally, hide the shoulder seams on the outside, which can be done in one of two ways. You can cover them with motifs that echo those already at the shoulders, or you can apply free-form shapes cut from the same fabrics that appear near the shoulders. Anchor and embellish these new pieces with free-motion stitching to blend in with the rest of the shoulder area. Your shoulder seams will disappear.

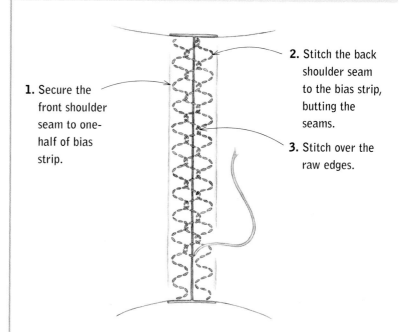

1. Secure the front shoulder seam to one-half of bias strip.

2. Stitch the back shoulder seam to the bias strip, butting the seams.

3. Stitch over the raw edges.

Butt the front shoulder seam to the back one, covering the second half of the bias strip, and stitch in place. Run a third row of stitching down the middle where the seams butt, holding both raw edges securely in place.

"All My Senses Sing Her": The right shoulder seam is camouflaged with floral motifs, the left with a self-fabric bias strip. *(Photo by Jack Deutsch.)*

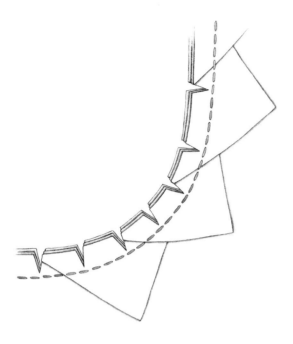

After the piping and triangle-shaped facings have been stitched to the right side of the outside edges, clip all curves just to the stitching. This will enable the curves to lie flat when the facing is flipped to the inside and stitched in place.

This is an example of free-motion satin stitching on a shaped edge. (*Photo by Jack Deutsch.*)

Finishing the Edges

The edges of your vest are now ready to be finished. There is a slight difference between finishing the edges of a vest and those of a wall hanging, which was described on pp. 59-66. A vest has curved edges at the neckline and around the armscye. These curves must be clipped to the stitching after the piping and facing are applied so that the seams will lie flat when the facing is turned to the inside (see the illustration at left).

When selecting a thread for finishing, choose a color that will blend in with the facings you'll be using, unless a strong color contrast will provide the drama that your design needs. Using the same thread in the bobbin as on the top will make it easier to deal with a machine that's temperamental about tension settings, but I've gotten good results using contrasting top and bobbin thread colors, too. Another interesting effect can be obtained by using variegated thread in the top and in the bobbin.

1 Begin by applying corded piping and triangle-shaped facings, as described on pp. 62-66, to all but the shaped edges of your vest, beginning and ending the stitching ¼ in. into the shaped edges. Be sure to clip the seam allowances in all curved areas to the stitching line, so the seams can be turned without stretching. Remember to empty the cording from the ends of the piping before sewing the piping onto the garment.

2 Using a 1.5mm stitch width, free-motion zigzag-stitch at the shaped edge, beginning and ending the stitching at the piped facing on either side and stitching right on the edge of your shaped motifs.

3 Trim away the excess fabric close to the stitching, then reset your machine to a 2.5mm-wide zigzag stitch. Free-motion stitch over the first row of stitching, this

Iridescent metallic
thread embellishes this
shaped edge. The final
pass of free-motion
stitching varies in width
from 2.5mm to 4mm.
*(Photo by Grey
Crawford.)*

time going ⅛ in. beyond the points
where the facing and cording end and
allowing the needle to stitch slightly off
the raw edge.

4 On the third and final pass, set the
stitch width to 3.5mm and free-motion
stitch forward and in reverse along ½ in. of
the edge at a time, building up an edge that
covers the remaining whiskers and that
looks corded (see the illustration at right).

5 If you're an experienced free-motion
sewer and enjoy a challenge, try varying
the width of your final stitching from
2.5mm to 4mm or wider, manipulating the
stitch-width control with your right hand
while guiding the fabric under the needle
with your left. This takes lots of practice and
eye-hand coordination, but the effect can be
spectacular.

6 Put your vest through one last run
through the short cycles on your washing machine and dryer to soften the edges
of the fabrics you've just added. Trim any
long, frayed threads even with the soft collaged edges, and you're ready to embellish
your vest with a nifty closure.

SATIN-STITCHING A SHAPED EDGE

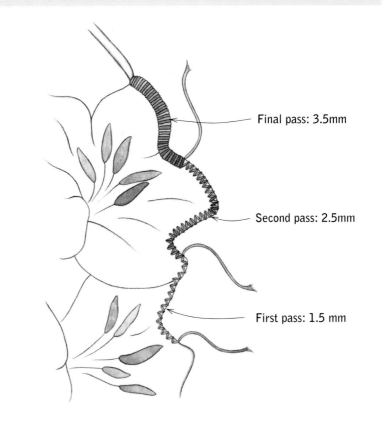

Final pass: 3.5mm

Second pass: 2.5mm

First pass: 1.5 mm

6
Collage for Outerwear

It's just a short step from making a collaged vest to using collage techniques on outer garments such as tunics, jackets, dusters, and coats. Unlike vests, however, these garments are not collaged on muslin. Instead, collage fabrics are sewn directly on selected areas of the fashion fabric. Another difference is that you'll have to tackle seam construction.

My design theme is typically inspired by a stunning fabric—often one that I've just acquired because it's the one I'm most excited about—and the choice of that fabric then affects the type of garment that I'll make, its style, the collage layout, and the other fabrics I'll use. However, I don't make these decisions in any particular order. I just keep open to ideas as they come to me, trying this fabric with that as I search through my stash, collecting just the right trims as they find me. Then I step aside and let my muses have their way with me.

Choosing a Pattern

Garments with pared-down, refined styling make the best showcases for fabric collage. The easiest patterns to use have few pieces, and their seams are straight lines. Since the collage is ideally applied to a flat surface, prime pattern choices are free of design details like darts, tucks, and gathers in the areas you intend to embellish.

TUNICS

A tunic is probably the simplest of these outer garments to collage. Its loose fit, flat surfaces, and absence of sleeves make it an excellent blank canvas for a beginning wearable-collage project. By varying a tunic's length and the fabrics you choose, you can create a tunic for every occasion from beach to ballroom. A long tunic—one that's almost to the floor—makes a dramatic

"Who Dwells Therein?": Simple styles with a minimum of seams and design lines make the best styles for artwear. Folkwear Pattern 118, the Tibetan Panel Coat, with all of the design seams eliminated, was used for this reversible tunic. *(Photo by Jack Deutsch.)*

your best pattern choice is one that has loose fit, large armholes, and extended shoulders with wide sleeves. This style gives you flat areas to sew on and easy access to the seams. When considering a pattern, look carefully at the shape of the pattern pieces, and choose a pattern that has large, smooth curves at the seamlines over one that has tight curves or sharp angles.

Jackets and coats with traditional set-in sleeves and close fit are more challenging but not impossible if you keep in mind that you must minimize the bulk created by collage. Because the cap of the sleeve must be eased to fit the armscye, you don't want it to be too heavy with many layers of collage. If you decide to work with set-in sleeves, use minimum collage on the sleeve construction area. The body of the garment must have a minimum of collage layers,

statement when worn over an ankle-length skirt or flowing palazzo pants. A mid- or thigh-length tunic of linen or textured cotton is a chameleon, adaptable to many occasions and flattering to women of all heights. The mid-calf-length tunic is also versatile; made of a natural fabric such as linen, it can be worn over jeans for a barbecue or over matching wide-legged pants for the theater.

COATS AND JACKETS

If you're undertaking a more ambitious project such as a collaged coat or jacket,

"Dragonflies Foiled Again": The fronts of this mid-length tunic are embellished with collaged appliqué and foil. Some of this foil, which is applied over a tacky glue made especially for it, may wash out in the final laundering, depending on the base fabric. *(Photo by Jack Deutsch.)*

too, or the armscye seam will become too bulky for wearing comfort. Making an unlined garment is another way to reduce bulk in the armscye.

Garments that have sleeves that are cut in one piece with the body are poor choices for collage. I like the idea: one large flat area to collage, with no construction seams except where the front joins the back on top of the sleeves, at the shoulders, and at the underarms. However, these sleeves are designed with fullness under the arm to facilitate movement. The extra weight of the collage in these areas would interfere with drape, causing the garment to be cumbersome and to bulge out at the armholes, both front and back.

If your heart is set on using a pattern with sleeves cut in one with the body, choose a fabric that isn't too stiff or crisp so that it will drape in front of and in back of the arms. Then keep the collage elements toward the center front and center back of the garment, using collage only on the top of the sleeve and shoulder in the arm area of the garment.

Finally, when you are first experimenting with collaged garments, your chances for success are better if you choose a pattern with a generous cut and loose fit. Unlike wall hangings and vests that are completely covered with collage, partly collaged garments don't necessarily shrink uniformly in the wash. The textured collaged areas are most likely to pucker and crinkle, while the uncollaged areas will be flatter and will shrink less. A generous cut makes it easier to make up for these inconsistencies.

KEEPING YOUR PATTERN SIMPLE

After choosing your pattern, think about whether you can simplify it even more: Are there any seams that just serve as design elements? If so, these seamlines can be matched and taped together to eliminate having to construct them.

"All My Senses Sing Her": This coat sports wide sleeves and armscyes that provide flat areas for collage and easy access to seams so they can be camouflaged. *(Photo by Jack Deutsch.)*

Center back seams are often straight or so close to straight that they can be eliminated without having a noticeable effect on fit and style. Sometimes center back seams are used on coats or tunics because a seamless back wouldn't fit on fabric of standard widths. Trimming 1 in. or so at the side seam will probably have little effect on the design and may narrow the back width enough to make it possible for you to cut

Fold

Original cutting line

Place the new center back on the fold of the fabric.

Original cutting line

Use the new cutting line if necessary on narrower fabrics.

"For a Rainy Spring Wedding": Chocolate bargello piecing, vintage drapery fabric, and ombre silk ribbons are some of the collaged elements on this ankle-length, herringbone, natural silk tunic. The hemline is fringed. *(Photo by Jack Deutsch.)*

the back as one piece (see the illustration above).

The side seams of some garments occasionally can be eliminated by taping together the pattern's front and back seam-lines under the arms. This usually requires cutting out the garment on the crosswise grain. For the fabric to drape similarly on both the crosswise and lengthwise grains, its warp (lengthwise threads running parallel to the selvage) and the weft (crosswise or fill-ing threads) must be balanced. In other words, the threads that make up the weave must be the same in size, twist, and fiber content. To check the balance, unravel a few of the threads from both directions in the weave and compare them. If they are the same, the weave is balanced, and the garment is likely to hang well when cut on the crosswise grain.

Even if the warp and weft aren't evenly balanced, you can often ignore the rule that says the grainline of the pattern must run parallel to the lengthwise grain of the fabric. Drape the fabric around your body with the crosswise grain running perpendicular to the floor to help you visualize how the fabric will work in your garment. If it still drapes well and doesn't pooch out as it falls from your bust or shoulders, you can cut it successfully on the crosswise grain. If your fabric has texture that is prominent in one direction such as a rib or slub, make sure you still like the effect when you change the direction of the grainline.

Finally, are there design details that can be eliminated? You may want to get rid of any details that detract from the overall effect of the collage, such as collars, cuffs, and front bands. Removing a collar then placing collage at the neckline of a coat or tunic will finish the edge and draw flattering attention to the face, just as a collar would have.

How Much Collage Is Too Much Collage?

You've no doubt noted that there's no need to collage the entire surface of a garment. In fact, wearing a full-length garment entirely collaged with three or four layers of fabric might feel like wearing a suit of armor. Therefore, after choosing a suitable fashion fabric for your garment, consider how to use collage as embellishment rather than as an allover surface design.

When I collage a tunic, I typically apply the collage on the shoulders and upper backs. For coats, I've collaged at the hemlines and front edges, with additional collage at the shoulders. I sometimes extend collage up the back of a coat from the hemline. A garment's yoke is another area that may inspire creativity.

"Humble Origins": This coat was the first garment on which I experimented with shaped edges. I used an inexpensive flannel as the base fabric and one piece of polished cotton drapery fabric for the collaged elements. Tiny silk piping is inserted between the saddle sleeves and the body of the coat. *(Photo by Jack Deutsch.)*

This duster features individual leaves that were layered on muslin and lining fabric. The leaves were sewn onto the lower edge of the yoke, but the lower edges of the leaves were left free to create a three-dimensional effect. *(Photo by Jack Deutsch.)*

Planning Placement of the Collage

When you start placing collage on your garment, a sketch will help you plan your design and can be used as a map. To make a sketch, trace your garment's silhouette, both the front and the back, from the pattern envelope. If the pattern envelope doesn't show the back, just trace the front view without the front closure and give it an appropriate back neckline. Include all seamlines in your drawings. If necessary, use a copy machine to enlarge your drawings to 6 in. to 8 in., then make six to eight copies so you can sketch different design ideas. You can also use tracing paper over your original enlarged copy. Save all your sketches; the

ones you don't use this time may inspire future projects.

As you sketch, remember that the viewer's eye will be attracted to the places where collage is applied. To draw attention to the person wearing the garment, place most of the collage around the shoulders to create a frame for the face. However, if you want the viewer to focus on the story your coat or tunic has to tell, use the full expanses of the back and fronts.

Use collage to create illusions. To give the effect of height, for instance, use vertical placement of collage on the front edges of a garment that's worn open. To narrow hips, place a band of collage up the front, which draws attention away from the hipline. Avoid horizontal bands of collage in the hip area, since that will emphasize width. Another slimming trick is to place collage diagonally across the body, which will create asymmetric balance as attention is drawn away from the hipline (see the illustration on the facing page).

Selecting Fabrics for Collaged Outerwear

What types of fabrics make really good choices for your collaged tunics and coats? Think of the plans you have for this particular garment when it's done. Maybe this will be the jacket you reach for each time you need to look sharp but are in too much of a hurry to do a creative wardrobe blitz. You'll want to choose a sturdy fabric in a color that won't show soil easily. Think denim, twill, heavy linen, flannel, and chino. Look in stores that sell fabrics for home decoration. There you'll find a broad range of heavy linens and textured cottons that work well for collage. I often use these

"Sunshine on My Shoulder": Bargello piecing creates the sunshine on this linen duster. The bargello's raw edges are covered with collage that extends down the back and over the opposite shoulder. *(Photo by Jack Deutsch.)*

Bands of collage up the front emphasize height.

Collage placed diagonally draws attention away from the hips.

fabrics unlined, as they have good body and work well for casualwear in my mild climate.

If you'll be making a stylish tunic that only comes out of the closet for weddings and holiday parties, good choices are medium-weight linen, silk noil or dupioni, and cotton damask or jacquard. You'll also get stunning effects using silk suiting fabrics with shots of metallic threads or other knots and slubs.

You may be thinking that you can use only unpatterned, smooth background fabrics for your collage. Plain weave linens, cottons, and silks *do* make good collage foundations, but I've also gotten impressive results designing on plaids, stripes, and textured fabrics. Exercise restraint when collaging on a heavily textured fabric, however, as the textured background makes a statement of its own that competes with the collage. The cliché "a little goes a long way" applies when you are combining collage and heavy textures.

When choosing a foundation fabric, visualize how it might look as background for your other fabrics. Your sketch will help your perceptions, especially if you attach samples of fabrics you're considering. Be sure to choose a color that you know looks good on you and that coordinates with the rest of your wardrobe.

Launderability must also be kept in mind when you select fabrics because you'll be

Sumptuous fabrics and subtle colors are good possibilities for collaged special-occasion outerwear. *(Photo by Grey Crawford.)*

Search stores that sell home-decorative fabrics for rich plaids, stripes, and sophisticated textures. *(Photo by Grey Crawford.)*

"Who Dwells Therein?": This tunic's raw silk, generously shot with lurex threads, required a minimum of collage. Using restraint in collaging allowed the elegance of the background fabric to make a statement. *(Photo by Jack Deutsch.)*

creating texture in the washing machine. That doesn't mean you have to shy away from the bolts marked "dry clean only." Textile manufacturers give these warnings to let you know that they can't be responsible for consumers' aberrant laundry practices.

If you like a fabric that's marked "dry clean only," buy ⅛ yd. of it to toss in with a load of laundry. You'll be pleasantly surprised to see the beautiful textures that are liberated when certain silks and other luxury fabrics have been laundered. And once these fabrics have been used for your collaged garment and laundered, they're unlikely to change when washed again.

PREPARING THE FABRIC

I always prewash my foundation and lining fabrics for coats, tunics, and jackets. Long lengths of denim, linen, silk—any fabric I might use—can shrink an undetermined amount, so I want that shrinkage under control before I lay out my collages.

After choosing your fabrics, preshrink them following the directions on pp. 56–58. Remove your yardage from the dryer while it is still slightly damp, smooth it flat with your hands, and let it air-dry. I prefer this hand-pressing method to ironing fabrics completely smooth because it leaves the finish the fabric will have when the garment is completed.

Constructing a Coat

It's a more complex project to tackle a collaged coat or jacket with its multiple

> ### By the Way
> Serge or use a short zigzag stitch on the cut ends of yardage before preshrinking it. You'll avoid the tangled mess that results when long weft threads unravel in your washing machine.

construction seams and larger surface than to make a seamless vest. But I find the satisfaction I experience when I've met the challenge is worth the extra effort. Just approach it one step at a time, knowing that your creative nature will help you solve any problems if they arise.

Whenever possible, follow your pattern's layout instructions when you cut out your garment. Be sure to add at least 1 in. beyond the normal ⅝-in. seam allowances for tunics, coats, and jackets.

Start by spreading out your largest pattern piece, usually the back, on a large work surface. You'll be working with several garment pieces, so you'll need your sketch near your workspace. I often stray from my sketched map, but I need it to get me started when I lay out the collage. As you did when you designed your vest or sample wall hanging, arrange the main elements of your collage first. You might find it helpful to refer back to the design principles on pp. 21-25 before you start.

When collaging on a fashion fabric, you no longer have to worry about overlapping each of the collage fabrics by ½ in. because you're not covering up every bit of muslin underlining as you did when making a vest or wall hanging. In fact, when the background fabric peaks out here and there around your motifs, you're creating negative shapes that become part of the collage (see pp. 16-19). You'll recall that negative spaces are the blank areas around your collage. Try making these shapes as interesting as the positive or motif shapes.

APPROACHING THE SEAMS

As your collage design approaches the seamlines where the next piece of the garment will be joined, such as where the front will be joined to the back at a side seam, lay these pieces next to one another so you can see how the designs on one piece will relate to those on the other. Remember that you have added an extra

1 in. beyond the cutting lines, so you'll need to keep your motifs about 1¾ in. away from the cut edges of your garment. Otherwise an important bird may lose his tail as it disappears into a seam.

Also, plan now for how you'll be camouflaging the seams with motifs after your garment has been sewn together. If you have a particular motif to place over a specific seam, set it aside now with a note pinned to it to remind you later where it's to be placed.

PLANNING SHAPED EDGES FOR OUTERWEAR

If you've chosen a loose-fitting style that doesn't have to be cut precisely to size, any

"Eventide Visitors": Open spaces in the body of this collage are interesting negative shapes created by the edges of the motifs around them. *(Photo by Jack Deutsch.)*

of its outer edges are good candidates for shaped edges. In fact, all its edges can be shaped, as they are on the coat in the photo on p. 97, for a playful look. Reread the directions for shaped edges on pp. 92-93 before you begin. As you design, let your motif's edges meander into the extra 1-in. margin. This will make up for shrinkage. Placing collage on the inside of sleeves' hemlines to create shaped edges gives you the option of turning up collaged cuffs.

FREE-MOTION EMBELLISHING THE GARMENT PIECES

Stand back and assess your design occasionally. When you're satisfied, use lots of pins to hold the collage in place. After

Motifs stitched to the lining side of this sleeve provide for an optional turned-back cuff. *(Photo by Grey Crawford.)*

pinning, hold the garment pieces next to one another with their seam allowance folded out of the way so you can see how they'll look when they're stitched at the seams. Make any design changes now if they're needed.

Then, following the instructions for free-motion sewing on pp. 50-55, embellish your collage. I usually stitch over the uncollaged areas of the background to give it textural interest and to equalize the shrinking of the collaged and uncollaged areas. If you decide to stitch the background, choose one of the stitching patterns shown in the illustration at left or invent one of your own.

If your garment will sport shaped edges, use free-motion sewing and either a straight stitch or a narrow (1.5mm) zigzag stitch to reinforce the outer edges of the motifs that will be your shaped edges. You'll be cutting as close as possible to this stitching after the garment pieces are washed.

When you're through with the free-motion stitching, use short, gentle wash and dry cycles to shrink and texture the garment pieces, taking them out of the dryer before they get bone dry. Then hand-press all of the garment pieces, and allow them to air-dry on a flat surface.

STITCHING PATTERNS

When embellishing a garment using free-motion sewing, you can use one of these stitching patterns or create one of your own.

TRIMMING THE GARMENT TO THE PATTERN

When it's time to trim the collaged garment pieces, a small rotary cutter is the best tool. It saves time, and its razor-sharp edge slices right through the multiple layers of fabric with incredible accuracy. Of course, you can use scissors, but if you've never cut out a garment with a rotary cutter, give it a try.

First, use the cutter to trim off the excess pattern paper beyond the seam allowances. Don't skip this step or you'll end up shredding your pattern when you try to cut through both the pattern and the fabric at the same time.

Next, lay the pattern on its corresponding collaged garment piece. If you've planned for shaped edges, arrange the pattern so that its cutting line lies along the innermost points of the motifs. The outermost points will extend beyond the edges of your paper pattern (see the illustration at right). The shaped edges shouldn't be trimmed to the pattern's edges. On shaped edges, use scissors to trim close to the line of reinforcing stitches, but stop trimming them a couple of inches away from the seams. You'll complete the trimming after the seams are stitched.

It isn't necessary to pin the pattern to the fabric—I use my large hardware store washers as weights to keep the pattern from shifting around. After the pattern is in place, trim next to the pattern's cutting line. Straight lines are a snap to cut by placing a ruler on the garment side of the cutting line to hold the fabric and pattern in place while you trim away the excess with a rotary cutter. Hold the ruler solidly in place so it won't slip off the cutting line, then use firm pressure on the cutter as you slowly roll the blade away from you.

Because fabric layers tend to push ahead of the rolling blade on curves, use your free hand to put pressure on the layers just behind the blade and hold them back. This slight resistance keeps layered fabric in place

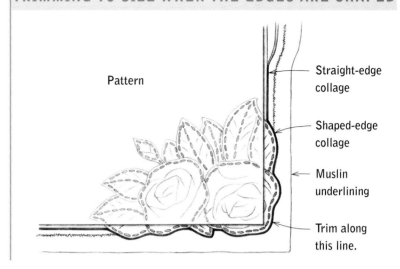

TRIMMING TO SIZE WHEN THE EDGES ARE SHAPED

Pattern

Straight-edge collage

Shaped-edge collage

Muslin underlining

Trim along this line.

so you can make a smooth cut. On tight curves, I press my fingertips into the fabric a little less than ¼ in. from the cutting line, then slowly and carefully make the cut. I haven't yet trimmed my fingernails with this maneuver, but I respect my rotary cutter and am exceptionally cautious.

To mark construction notches, just lift the pattern above the notches and mark them with a water-soluble marking pen. You could also use small, colored pressure-sensitive dots from a stationery store. I use the same method to mark match points such as those on sleeve-cap seams and yokes.

CHOOSING A SEAM FINISH

The seams I use on my outerwear garments are the butted seam, Hong Kong-finished seam, bias-covered seam, bound-standing seam, and faced seam. I'm not committed to using these seams exclusively, so don't hesitate to use a favorite of your own—or

By the Way

By first pressing seams flat, the way they're sewn, it's then easier to press them open.

invent one. You will, however, need to think through the construction of your garment and decide on your seam finishes before you begin. Often my experience tells me when a certain seam may be most appropriate, but when it's not obvious to me which will work best, I make samples.

Butted seam This is the seam I use at the shoulders of vests (see detailed directions on pp. 90-91). Briefly, its construction involves covering a seam with a layer of fabric on each side of the garment. I use a ¾-in. bias strip of a firmly woven fabric as an underlayer on the inside of the garment, and on the outside I use motifs or shapes cut from the same fabrics that I used in the collage. Since the seam allowances are removed, this seam treatment is very flat. When many layers of collaged fabric are involved at the seamline, the butted seam is a good choice.

A butted seam is especially appropriate for short seams such as those at the shoulders or set-in sleeves if the sleeve cap is straight or very shallow. A butted seam, camouflaged with collage, gives the appearance of seamless construction, which is quite puzzling to the viewer. I like that!

Since it takes four or more steps to complete a butted seam, I rarely use it on extended seams such as the long side seams of coats and tunics. It's impossible to use this seam for the underarm seams of most sleeves unless the sleeves are extremely large. There's just not enough room inside

most sleeves to do the stitching required to finish a butted seam.

Hong Kong-finished seam A Hong Kong-finished seam is a normal seam in that it is sewn with right sides together and pressed open, but then each raw edge is bound with its own bias strip. The Hong Kong finish is traditionally used on seams for couture and luxury garments. My collaged garments use a number of traditional techniques in nontraditional ways, and this is one of my favorites for unlined garments that are not reversible. A skillfully executed seam finish adds a touch of luxury to a garment and presents an interesting detail to anyone who glimpses the inside.

For bias strips, I like to use small stripes or tiny prints that relate to the colors of the main fabric or the collage fabrics in my garment. But I also like the fabric to have an element of surprise, so I look for lightweight fabrics that contrast in value and texture to the background fabric exposed in the seams.

1 To construct a Hong Kong-finished seam, sew the seam as usual with right sides together and press open.

2 For every seam to be finished, cut two bias, or off-grain, strips 1¼ in. wide and as long as the seam itself. (See p. 61 for more information about cutting and joining bias strips.)

3 Aligning the raw edges, sew a bias strip face down to the right side of one seam allowance at ¼ in. Use a rotary cutter to trim this seam allowance to ⅛ in.

4 Press the bias strip binding toward the raw edge, fold it over that edge to the wrong side, and press.

5 On the right side of the seam, keeping the binding free of the body of your garment, stitch in the ditch along your previous stitching line to secure the binding's raw edge (see the left illustration on the facing page).

"For a Rainy Spring Wedding": A traditional band with topstitching finishes the neckline and front edges of this long tunic. *(Photo by Jack Deutsch.)*

A seam's raw edges are bound with a lightweight bias strip to create a fine finishing detail.

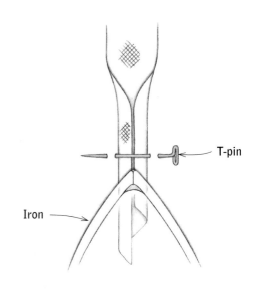

6 Finally, trim the raw edge of the binding on the underside close to the stitching. This is easiest to do using duck-billed appliqué scissors. Repeat for the other half of the seam allowance.

Single-fold bias-covered seam This method presents a seam that is neatly hidden by a length of single-fold bias strip. A bias-covered seam can be used for garments that are constructed from closely woven, sturdy fabrics such as linen or denim. It is a very attractive finish for the side seams and the underarm sleeve seams of reversible garments. When the bias is cut from a contrasting fabric, the seam becomes a decorative detail. This seam finish is not practical, however, for seams on loosely woven fabrics because the seam allowance is trimmed short and could pull out.

1 To make a bias-covered seam, stitch a normal seam with right sides together using a slightly shorter-than-normal stitch (8 to 10 stitches per inch).

2 Trim both seam allowances at the same time to ¼ in. using a rotary cutter. Press open.

By the Way

In the absence of a bias-tape maker, you can improvise one using a long T-pin on your ironing board (see the above right illustration). The pin should catch the ironing-board cover in two places so that the exposed length of pin between them is ½ in. long. You can then guide your tape under this length of pin, pressing it as it comes through.

3 From a lightweight and firmly woven fabric, cut one bias strip for each seam 1⅛ in. wide and the length of the seam to be covered.

4 Using a ½-in. bias-tape maker, press the bias as you pull it through so that the two raw edges meet in the middle of the tape. I strongly advise investing a few dollars in one of these useful gadgets since life is too short for us to iron yards of bias strips without aids. Don't bother using purchased single-fold bias. The color choices and the quality of the fabrics don't meet the standards of custom-made artwear.

5 Glue-baste or pin the bias strip over the open seam and edgestitch each side of

A single-fold bias-strip covering gives a neat, flat finish to straight or slightly curved seams.

Back side

Both raw seam edges are enclosed in one bias strip to make a bound seam that stands up. On a reversible garment, this seam becomes a dramatic design element.

the strip in place (see the above left illustration). Both rows of stitching must be sewn in the same direction so that the bias strip won't be pulled askew. Use a walking foot, if you have one, for this task.

Raw-edged bias-covered seam A bias-covered seam with even less bulk and a more casual look can be made by centering a strip of raw-edged bias over the pressed-open seam.

1 Begin by cutting a bias strip just ⅝ in. wide, and glue-baste or pin it to cover the seam.

2 Use a row of straight stitching or a narrow zigzag down the middle of the strip to hold it in place.

3 Next, use free-motion stitching to meander over the surface of the bias strip, catching its raw edges as you stitch it in place. Because the strip has been cut on the bias, its edges won't ravel but they'll soften, keeping in character with collage.

A similar treatment can be used on straight or nearly straight seams where bias isn't required to accommodate curves. For these strips, you can use ribbon, decora-

tive trims, lightweight suede, or synthetic suede. Woven fabrics cut on the straight grain can also be used like single-fold bias strips in the previous method. Just cut the strips the desired width plus two ¼-in. seam allowances. For a ¾-in. finished strip, cut the strip 1¼ in. wide, then press under ¼ in. on each side.

Bound-standing seam This seam stands on end and is reinforced and sturdy because the binding is stitched through both seam allowances on top of the stitched seam. The garment's seam is not pressed open, but rather the seam edges are bound as one. This finish is appropriate for seams with collage extending into the seam allowance, where there is a bulky seam that's difficult to press open. If you decide to use it for reversible garments, keep in mind that this seam will stand away from the garment and become a noticeable decorative detail.

1 Start by placing the right sides of the garment together, then sew on the seamline and trim the allowances to ¼ in. using a rotary cutter. (see the above right illustration).

A bound-standing seam finishes the sleeve on the inside of a reversible garment. *(Photo by Grey Crawford.)*

2 Press the seam flat the way it was sewn.

3 Next, cut bias binding strips 1¼ in. wide and the length of the seams to be finished. You'll need one bias strip for each seam.

4 Laying the bias strip face up, align one of its raw edges with those of the seam.

5 Stitch the strip to the seam along the seam's original stitching line.

6 Wrap the bias binding around the raw edges of the seam allowance.

7 Then turn under the binding's raw edge so its fold lies along the stitching line and completely encloses the seam's raw edges. You can stitch this down by hand or machine.

8 If folding the binding under to finish it on the second side makes the seam too bulky, don't fold it under. Instead, wrap it snugly over the raw edges, pin it flat on the top side, then machine-stitch in place by stitching in the ditch, once again following the stitching line of the original seam. One side of the strip will be neatly folded under and the other will have a raw edge.

9 Trim the raw edge of the bias binding about ⅛ in. from the line of stitching. Since this is a bias raw edge, it won't ravel in the laundry but will instead form a soft edge like those on your collage.

Faced seam You may not be familiar with the faced-seam finish because it's one that I've created as a solution to completing collaged garments that have facings around the armscye, around necklines, and at front edges. This is one of my favorite finishes to use on collaged sleeveless tunics because it's easy, it finishes the edges of both the facings and the seams in one step, and it works for either lined or unlined garments. I use the term finish loosely because these seams and facings aren't really finished. Instead, they have soft raw edges, just like those of a collage.

1 To prepare your pattern for this easy seam and facing, clearly mark on the side seamline of both the front and the back the spot that indicates where the stitching begins for the underarm seam. If your tunic has slits at the hemline, mark the spot where they begin.

2 Tape this side of your pattern to a 6-in.-wide strip of pattern paper that is the full length of the garment from the shoulder to the hemline.

3 Next, mark new cutting lines for self-facings by measuring 1½ in. from the seamline at the armscye (and side slit) and ¾ in. from the side seams. Mark an easy curve connecting the facings to the side seams (see the illustration below).

ALTERING THE PATTERN FOR FACED SEAMS

New cutting line

Original cutting line

New 1½-in. self-facing

New ¾-in. seam allowance

New 1½-in. self-facing

Tunic front

Make the same alteration on the pattern back-side seam.

This topstitching was actually done with a twin needle from the opposite side of the garment. Twin needles create a tiny zigzag stitch on the bobbin side that holds a decorative cord in place. *(Photo by Grey Crawford.)*

4 For your garment's neckline and front facings, retain the seam allowances that will be stitched to the neckline and front edges, but change the width of the facing to 1½ in.

5 To construct the garment, sew the side seams between the marks with right sides together.

6 Press the seam open, then continue pressing the foldlines of the armhole and side-slit facings.

7 Join the neckline and front facings to each other and then to the garment with right sides together.

8 Press and pin or glue-baste the facings in place.

9 Finally, topstitch the facings ⅛ in. from their raw edges. Start the topstitching at the shoulder, then stitch down toward the hem at both the front and the back of the garment. At the neckline, begin topstitching at the center back and stitch toward the hem at the opening edge of the front.

This topstitching can also be done with a narrow (1.5mm) zigzag stitch or with twin needles (see the top photo at left). If you choose to use twin needles, insert a 2mm

twin needle into your sewing machine, then feed a cord of perle cotton, small rayon yarn, or other smooth, decorative cord up through the hole in the machine's faceplate from its underside. The twin needles will create a tiny zigzag stitch on the bobbin side that holds the cord in place.

This faced-seam treatment can also be constructed by first sewing wrong sides of the garment together, then pressing the facings and seams toward the right side. The seams and facings become a decorative element on the right side of the garment (see the bottom photo at left).

If these seam finishes are new to you, make samples so you'll be able to feel them as well as see what they look like. Samples will help you make decisions on which finishes to use on your garments. It's not necessary to use the same seam finish throughout the garment.

Constructing an Unlined Sleeveless Tunic

Tunics with simple styling easily lend themselves to being canvases for artwear because they have an expanse of uncluttered surface just waiting to be adorned.

1 After you've preshrunk your background fabric, cut out the pattern with 1-in. shrinkage allowance on all sides except the shoulder seams. Cut and sew normal shoulder seams, then finish them using one of the methods just described.

2 Clean-finish the raw edges with a serger so they'll remain intact as you handle and launder the fabric. In the absence of a serger, staystitch ¼ in. from the raw edges.

3 Next, stretch your tunic out flat on a large work surface and design your collage. Because the shoulder seams are already stitched, you can create an uninterrupted

This tunic's side seams, armscye, side-slit facings, and pocket facing were all applied to the inside of the garment then pressed to the right side where they were topstitched in place with a twin needle. Raw edges were left to create a velvety finish. *(Photo by Jack Deutsch.)*

COLLAGING A TUNIC WITH THE SHOULDERS STITCHED

With the shoulders stitched, you can sew an uninterrupted collage from front to back.

flow of collage from the back of the tunic, over the shoulders, and cascading down the fronts (see the illustration above). Avoid making more than one layer of collage where the side seams will be; you can add more layers after these seams are stitched.

4 Using free-motion stitching, embellish the collage. I'm especially particular about my choice of bobbin thread when making an unlined garment because it becomes the only embellishment on the inside. You can select a bobbin thread that blends in with the base fabric and creates only texture on the inside, but it's a lot more exciting to choose a thread that contrasts with the fabric, either in value or in texture. The plaid linen tunic shown in the

photo below is stitched predominantly with Sliver metallic thread in the bobbin.

5 For more texture, stitch the background fabric surrounding the collage (see p. 104 for stitching suggestions). As a guideline, there's no need to stitch on a background fabric that has lots of texture such as a handwoven fabric—the stitching would get lost in the texture. Background stitching will, however, enhance a less-textured fabric such as linen or denim and ensure overall shrinkage and texture.

6 When the collage and embellishment stitching is completed, launder and dry the garment using short, gentle cycles. Then lay your tunic out flat so you can trim it to match the pattern pieces.

7 Stitch and finish the side seams using any of the suggestions described in the previous section.

8 If you like, pipe and face the front and neckline edges (see pp. 59-66). Banded or shaped edges are also good choices for front and neckline edges.

"Eventide Visitors": Sliver metallic thread is the only embellishment on the inside of this tunic. *(Photo by Jack Deutsch.)*

**"Friendly Encounter":
For a collaged coat,
choose a pattern with
simple design lines and
easy access to seams for
finishing.** *(Photo by Jack
Deutsch.)*

heavier fabrics and longer garments. It's
sometimes hard to remove the weft from
lightweight fabrics, so I typically stop the
fringe at about 1 in. on linen and other
smooth, woven fabrics.

1 To fringe your tunic, have someone
mark the finished length of your garment, including the fringe.

2 Next, sew a narrow (1.5mm) zigzag
staystitch parallel to the bottom edge
where you intend the fringe to stop.

3 Pull out the weft (filler) threads up to
the staystitching. Unless your staystitching is perfectly on the grainline, which is
unlikely, the weft threads you're pulling out
will stop at the staystitched line midway
across the hemline.

4 Snip off the weft where it's held by the
staystitching, then pull out the next
weft thread, repeating until your fringe is
complete.

9 Because traditional hems on collaged
garments may be bulky and aren't
very interesting, try finishing them with
collaged shaped edges or with piped and
faced edges.

ADDING FRINGE

Adding fringe is another alternative for
finishing your tunic's hemline if it isn't
collaged. Fringe can be made from most
woven fabrics, but to see if you like the
effect with your fabric, it's important to
make a sample. Fringe made from some
lightweight fabrics and blends turns to fluff
or becomes a tangled mess in the laundry.
Heavy fabrics, such as textured linen, and
those with loose weaves, such as homespun
or monk's cloth, are easy to fringe and are
substantial.

A good length for fringe on most fabrics
is 1 in. to 2 in. Use the longer length for

**"Trip to Hong Kong": Simple shield shapes embellish
one side of this reversible tunic.** *(Photo by Jack
Deutsch.)*

Camouflaging Seams

Collaging over your seams on the right sides of your garments will create some mystery around the construction techniques you've used and will result in a finely crafted garment.

1 Bring out the motifs you've designated to cover your seams, or choose motifs that are related to those at the side seams.

2 After pinning the motifs in place, use the same style of free-motion stitching used on the rest of the collage to stitch their edges and embellish them.

3 Unless you've used a bias-covered side-seam finish to cover the seam allowances, take extra precautions to keep your finished seam allowances where they belong. I either glue-baste them in place or carefully pin them down from the right side of the garment. Don't place pin-basting on the seam allowance side of your garment or the pins will be impossible to avoid as you free-motion stitch from the right side.

4 Once the sewing is finished, give your tunic one last short trip through the laundry process (see pp. 57–58), and it's ready for a classy closure.

"Hopeful Cupid": A 1-in. fringe finishes the bottom of this light-weight linen tunic. *(Photo by Jack Deutsch.)*

Free-motion stitching attaches motifs that cover and camouflage seams after the final construction and seam finishing is completed. *(Photo by Grey Crawford.)*

7

Linings Alive:
Enhancing the
Other Side of Artwear

Most of my collaged garments are
reversible, and I think of both
sides as being important when I
am creating them. Even though the inside is
typically less complex, featuring just a little
soft-edge appliqué or a bit of traditional
piecing, I would rather not use phrases like
"the collaged side" and "the noncollaged
side" when I write directions. So, for
simplification, I'm calling the collaged side
the outside and the other side the lining.

Linings are used on the inside of clothing
to provide warmth, to conceal construction,
and to extend a garment's wear. A lining
can make outerwear more comfortable by
protecting the wearer from an abrasive fashion fabric. Clothes with sleeves are easier to
slip on and off when they are lined with a
slippery fabric. Slick linings keep outerwear
from sticking to the soft fabrics of other
garments. Linings also improve shape reten-

tion when used in garments constructed of
soft, stretchy fabrics.

On a different note, linings can be used
on the inside of artwear to provide an additional canvas for expression or to tell "the
other side of the story." A garment with a
lining that expresses a theme doesn't necessarily have to be reversible. The embellished
lining can simply be a surprise to be discovered on close examination.

As you've seen, all of my collaged vests
are lined and reversible. Some of my outerwear garments are lined but not necessarily
reversible. And some aren't lined at all but
are simply embellished by the novelty
threads I've used in the bobbin when doing
free-motion stitching. Whether or not a
lined garment is reversible, I plan for the
inside to complement the whole. This
chapter will offer suggestions for enhancing
linings that, I hope, will foster more
creative ideas.

(Photo opposite by Grey Crawford; photo above by Jack Deutsch.)

To Line or Not to Line

To help you decide if you should line your garment, you must first ask yourself some practical questions.

WILL YOU NEED AN EXTRA LAYER OF FABRIC FOR WARMTH?

Whether you line outerwear often depends on the climate in which you'll be wearing it. Even a lightweight silk lining may add just enough warmth to make your garment more comfortable—or less if you're wearing it in the tropics.

Even if a garment isn't going to be worn with the inside out, give the viewer of artwear a surprise when she peeks inside. *(Photo by Jack Deutsch.)*

DO YOU NEED A LINING TO MAKE THE GARMENT EASY TO SLIP INTO?

Some fabrics, such as velvet, corduroy, and soft woolens, tend to cling if they're worn over other soft fabrics, so a smooth lining can make a coat easier to put on and take off. Adding a smooth lining just to the sleeves is sometimes all you need to do. If you decide on this solution, choose a very lightweight lining such as a good-quality China silk that won't make the drape of the fabric in the sleeves appreciably different from the drape in the rest of the garment.

Luxurious fashion fabrics make beautiful linings for collaged outerwear. *(Photo by Grey Crawford.)*

HOW HEAVY WILL YOUR GARMENT BE IF IT'S LINED?

Sometimes artwear becomes heavy from all of the layers of fabric and embellishment we use. The best way I've found to gauge how heavy my unmade garment will become when it's finished is to unroll from the fabric bolts the approximate yardage required for both the lining and the foundation fabrics. Then hold the two fabrics together in the middle, and lift them as though they were a coat hanging on a hook. (The amount of fabric I'll add to collage a garment is about equal to the amount of fabric I'll remove when I cut out my garment.) If the fabrics feel too heavy, I'll look for a lining fabric that's lighter in weight, I'll line only the sleeves, or I'll eliminate the lining entirely.

Selecting a Lining Fabric

When I look for fabrics to line my collaged garments, I don't go to traditional lining fabrics. Lining garments for artwear gives you permission to use a wider range of linings than you're likely to choose for traditional garments. If your lining isn't planned to make your garment reversible, consider using a printed fabric. I find prime lining candidates among lightweight cotton and linen drapery fabrics. Top-quality fashion fabrics in silk and cotton and high-quality rayons also make superb linings.

Linings can be made from more than just one fabric, so take a look at remnant tables and your own stash to be inspired. An assortment of ½-yd. to 1-yd. remnants can be pieced to create a new fabric from which to cut your lining.

For a lining that you're going to paint, you'll need to use a natural fiber. Nothing beats silk such as dupioni, China silk, and jacquard for accepting textile paints. You can also paint on viscose rayon. Lightweight linen, linen/cotton blends, and high-quality cotton poplin are some other fabrics that I've painted successfully, but bear in mind that these fabrics are heavier than silk and will add more weight to the finished piece. They also take more time to heat-set. Mid- to light-value colors are easier to paint on. A dark-colored lining requires an opaque paint that's specifically made for dark fabrics.

Flat Lining a Collaged Garment

When I line a collaged garment, I normally use a method that is similar to underlining that's called flat lining. Simply, the lining and the fashion fabrics are cut out identically, then the corresponding pieces are stacked and basted together with wrong sides facing each other. The two pieces of fabric are handled as one when assembling the garment. You'll create an attractively lined and finished garment by flat lining, then finishing the seams using one of the methods described on pp. 105–110. If your garment's also to be reversible, finish it either with bias-covered seams or faced seams.

Embellishing Linings

There are a variety of embellishing techniques that are appropriate for using on linings but that are not exclusively for linings. For instance, you may find places where you'd like to use Afghani piecing on the outside of garments. For a really quick project, you can add soft-edge appliqué to an otherwise unadorned garment. Other ways to decorate the inside of your garment include lining a shaped edge, piecing a lining, making a medallion, and using bargello piecing. You could also embellish your lining by using interesting bobbin thread and even painting your lining.

ADDING A SOFT-EDGE APPLIQUÉ

Soft-edge appliqué is an easy way to introduce a hint of embellishment on the lining of an artwear garment. It creates a jazzy focal point for the lining that's especially effective when you plan to make your garment reversible.

A single soft-edge appliquéd rose is the simple embellishment—and the signature—on one vest's lining. (*Photo by Jack Deutsch.*)

An Inside Story

I believe that we create everything, whether it's a collage or a cake, from our inside—or soul side—out. So designing a garment's lining is a metaphor of my creative process. I consider the lining to be an integral part of the garment rather than as a necessary but incidental afterthought. That's why I try to design my linings to be interesting and evocative, even when the garment isn't intended to be reversible.

After creating collages for several years, I realized that I was often designing the linings of my vests and tunics first. It's easier for me to make a simple statement on the lining first because it lets me explore my ideas before I commit myself to a plan for the outside.

It's nonthreatening, and it gives me an opportunity to do something while I'm waiting to see what happens next.

What I've discovered by working this way is that my collage designs seem to find me, then they'll let me develop them if I'll just commit to starting the work. I may have only a kernel of an idea inspired by a fabric or an event. I'll begin to explore that idea while I'm working on the lining. When I cut and arrange those few lining fabrics, more ideas will come to me. By the time I've finished the lining, I have a better concept of the garment's story and which fabrics and colors I'll use to develop the idea more completely.

"Out of Africa It Ain't": This quill pen's feather began life as a leaf. Isolated from its original fabric and with the addition of a stitched pen point, it became the writing tool for the author's signature. *(Photo by Jack Deutsch.)*

Perhaps telling you the story of the vest I worked on as I wrote this book will help you see how this works.

I've been writing all day, organizing and reorganizing my ideas. I've definitely hit a blank

Designing a garment's lining is a metaphor of my creative process.

wall. Now it's time to think about making dinner, and there's no way I can handle the task, not even on autopilot. I have no decision-making brain cells left. I'm an artist, not a writer. What ever made me think I could write a book, and why did I think it would be such a great life experience, anyway? Must have been a total lapse of judgement.

I'd better shift gears before I do something rash—like throw in the towel on this writing project! I'll let my husband Ron worry about dinner. That's good. It gives me another hour to work. I guess I did have one decision-making cell left. Maybe I'll indulge myself and start a vest that I can use in the class I'll be teaching in a few days. That's my problem! I haven't had a chance to sew for two months. I'm obviously deep in the throes of sewing deprivation.

Green—that's all I can think of. I can always create if I work with green. Green heals and nurtures. Green is the color of my garden. I don't have any idea what to design. Maybe I'll just go garden instead. No, it's cold out there. I gardened yesterday. I need to handle fabric—green fabric. I pull from my stash every green batik fabric I own, plus another interesting green fabric that I recently rescued from a sale table. What a great green that sale fabric is! I love the whimsical metallic copper diamond shapes marching across its surface. I wonder why no one else liked it. It's probably ugly and I don't even know it. It's a good thing I'm saving it from oblivion. I like it, even if no one else does.

I arbitrarily choose one of the batik pieces that I think looks good with my copper-studded beauty. This is an astonishing change of pace. I can feel my blood start to circulate again. I cut several large pieces of the greens I've selected and arrange them to cover the muslin. Too boring. Needs something else—another green. I'm still not functioning at full power, but I'm breathing deeper. I'll recover.

My eye falls on a fabric that waits nearby on my design table. Bright birds and vivid flowers catch my eye, but once it's in my hands, it's the large leaves dyed green with

My eye falls on a fabric that waits nearby on my design table.

watercolor splotches of deep red-violet and aquamarine that I cut out. I like the singular shape of this leaf and its colors. I'll just use this leaf to embellish the lining, then I can get on with the real collage on the outside. I'm recovering my decision-making capabilities!

I try placing the leaf on the front, over the shoulder, on the side back—but it doesn't

look right anywhere. I'll see what it looks like with its stem pointed down instead of trying to tuck the stem under one of the green fabrics. Now it looks like a feather. And the black lines on that batik look like pen scribbles. Yesssss! I can make a quill pen out of my leaf-turned-feather, and it can be responsible for drawing the scribbled lines.

I'm really getting into this now. Dinner's been long forgotten. As I continue working on the lining, the feather pen reminds me of the writing project I've laid aside. It's not a glamorous task. My current writing project isn't anything like Isak Dinesen must have experienced when she was writing *Out of Africa*: all that glamour, the recollections of drama and romance…. That's it! That's what this vest is all about! My writing task is a challenge, sometimes hard work, and not the least bit glamorous. Not like writing *Out of Africa*. Thank you, Fabric Muse, for the insight! I'll do a fanciful African Savannah theme. I'll use my favorite Alexander Henry zebra fabric, my English cabbage-rose fabrics, and those fabrics that have words and letters on them. And I'll call it "Out of Africa, It Ain't!"

End of my frustration, beginning of a vest— and back to my writing with a fresh outlook.

"Out of Africa It Ain't" was inspired by the author's experiences writing this book. The closure sports a Jean Keeshin button. *(Photo by Jack Deutsch.)*

Soft-edge appliqué is collage's first cousin because of its raw edges that are fluffed by laundering. The difference between soft-edge appliqué and collage is that soft-edge appliqué is made up of individual motifs that are isolated like islands on the surface of the cloth. These motifs are often stitched only at their edges. Fabric collage, on the other hand, consists of raw-edged fabric pieces that are overlapped and stitched down. Fabric collage is usually embellished with sewing over its entire surface.

Soft-edge appliqué is done on the lining just before the lining is basted to the fashion fabric.

1 To create a simple soft-edge appliqué, select one or more motifs that relate to the theme of your garment.

2 Cut the motifs out, just as you did for collage, leaving a ⅛-in. margin around their edges.

3 Next, decide where you'd like to place the motifs (see the illustration at left for suggestions). Avoid placing them any closer than 2½ in. from the edges of your lining or you may lose your bird's beak when your garment is trimmed to the pattern or when you add the facings.

A minimum of soft-edge appliqué enhances this striped lining. The lining was cut in two pieces, with seam allowances added to the extra shrinkage allowance at center back, to create the interesting layout of angled stripes. *(Photo by Grey Crawford.)*

LINING A SHAPED EDGE

If you planned for the outer edges of your garment to be shaped by the outlines of some of the motifs placed at the edges, you can echo those shapes on the inside of your vest as well. Of course, the easiest thing to do is to use a single piece of fabric for the lining and finish it with an undulating edge of satin stitching. But it's fun to match that shaped edge with motifs on the inside of the garment, too.

1 Begin by cutting a lining that's identical to the outside of the garment. I use the collaged muslin as the pattern for cutting my lining.

LINING OPTIONS

2 From the outside of the garment, sew a very narrow zigzag stitch or a straight stitch to mark the outermost edges of the motifs (see the illustration at right). The bobbin thread of this stitching will be your guide for applying motifs to the lining.

3 Resist the temptation to trim the excess fabric from the edges just yet. You may need it to fudge the design a bit because it's unlikely that you'll find motifs that match perfectly the ones you've used on the outside of the garment.

4 Next, cut out motifs to use on the lining, then match their edges to the bobbin thread tracing at the outer edges as well as you can (see the illustration below). Since you've lined the garment to the edges, the lining will fill in any gaps that aren't covered by motifs that don't match perfectly.

5 Finally, finish the shaped edges following the directions on pp. 92-93.

MAKING PIECED LININGS

Pieced linings are a great way to use remnants from favorite sewing projects and fabric purchased that are just too small for entire garments.

1 To piece a lining, start by choosing fabrics that are compatible in weight.

2 Cut large, random-sized rectangles from your various fabrics, cutting the blocks on the straight grain.

3 Spread out your pattern pieces, and arrange your fabric blocks to cover them.

4 Next, join the fabrics together using conventional seams, pressing each seam open as you sew.

5 When you've created a new fabric large enough to fit your pattern piece, cut it

Muslin underlining

Use a narrow (1mm) zigzag stitch to mark the outermost edges of the motifs.

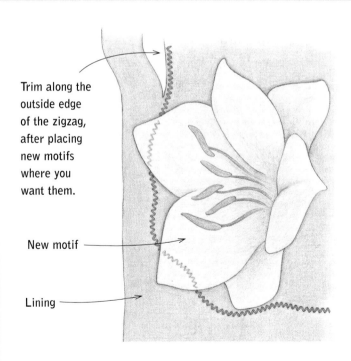

Trim along the outside edge of the zigzag, after placing new motifs where you want them.

New motif

Lining

The bobbin-thread zigzag marks the outer edge of the collage on the opposite side.

"Touched by an Angel": Linings can be pieced from several fabrics, with or without the addition of soft-edge appliqué. *(Photo by Jack Deutsch.)*

A bit of Afghani piece-work is nestled among collaged motifs on this vest's lining. *(Photo by Jack Deutsch.)*

out, being sure to include an extra 1-in. margin to allow for shrinkage.

If you're a quilter, here's an opportunity to use sample quilt blocks or class experiments that you've been hanging on to. If you have a fabric you'd like to use that's too narrow for your pattern piece, cut it in half lengthwise. Next, piece a long strip that's wide enough to make up the difference, and sew it between the two long pieces before you cut out the pattern. This works especially well for the center back of a garment. You may design a lining so appealing that you'll want to use your pieced lining to make your garment reversible.

USING AFGHANI PIECING

Afghani piecing is made up of stacked triangles that are framed by narrow fabric strips (see the photo at left below). Although this piecework appears to be the result of hours of sewing, it actually goes quickly once you've learned the trick of it. I've discovered that a 5-in.-wide strip of Afghani piecing inserted lengthwise into the middle of a yard of 45-in.-wide fabric makes a new piece of yardage that's wide enough to accommodate my vest pattern (see the top illustration on the facing page). Afghani piecing works great for this strip and is lots of fun to do. For your first time using this technique, make the straight Afghani strip I'm about to describe. Later you may want to try one of its variations.

In its simplest expression, Afghani piecing is created from two contrasting fabrics. When you choose your two fabrics, bear in mind that the beauty of the design will be lost if you use two busy, distinctive prints or if you use fabrics similar in value and without much contrast. A large, bold print is also a questionable choice because so little of it will show. For making a sample, choose a solid-colored fabric and one with a small allover print, a small-scale print, or one with contrasting texture such as an iridescent taffeta. You could also use a tiny motif fabric and a small-scale stripe.

To make a sample of Afghani piecing, you'll need:

- A strip of muslin backing that is 5 in. wide and 10 in. long

- A transparent template in the shape of an equilateral triangle that is 1¾ in. in height with sides roughly 2 in. long (see the template pattern in the bottom illustration at right).

- Fabric triangles, cut by using your template (see the following instructions)

- Two strips of contrasting fabric that are 1½ in. wide and about 45 in. long

To make the triangles, use a rotary cutter to cut a strip of fabric 1¾ in. wide. (Later, you may wish to vary the scale of your triangles. The width of the strip you cut them from will always equal the height you want your triangles to be.) Place the base of your template along the edge of the strip, and cut out triangles with a rotary cutter. By always laying the base of the template along the same side of the strip, you'll cut out two triangles with each cut (see the illustration on p. 124).

By stacking two or three strips on top of each other, you'll quickly cut out all the triangles you'll need for a long band of Afghani piecing. Alternately, you can trace the triangles with a fine-tipped water-soluble marking pen, then cut them apart with scissors. But since the rotary cutter method is so efficient, it's worth a few minutes' practice to master it.

Lining fabric 45-in. width

Selvage

Selvage

Pattern

22½ in.

22½ in.

Afghani piecing inset

AFGHANI PIECEWORK TEMPLATE

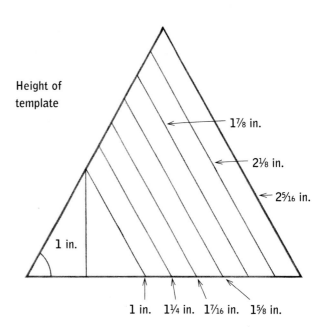

Height of template

1⅞ in.

2⅛ in.

2⁵⁄₁₆ in.

1 in.

1 in.   1¼ in.   1⁷⁄₁₆ in.   1⅝ in.

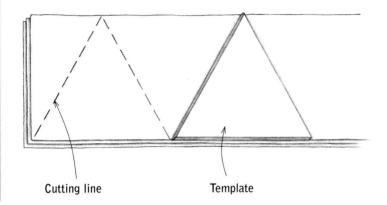

CUTTING TWO TRIANGLES WITH EACH CUT

Cutting line   Template

The width of the contrasting side strips should be in scale with your triangles. I make the strips' width equal to the triangles' height but never narrower than 1¼ in., even when I'm using triangles that are shorter than 1¼ in. Anything narrower is just too difficult to sew. The strips will be easiest to handle and to sew if they are cut on the lengthwise grain of the fabric. If you're using a vertical stripe, the strips must be cut on the lengthwise grain. However, since I have just quarter-yard pieces of many of my fabrics, I cut them on the crosswise grain and sew carefully, taking care to avoid stretching the strips.

1 To make your Afghani piecing sample, use a fabric marker to draw a guideline down the center of your backing strip.

2 Pinch-mark the midpoint of one side of a triangle, and consider this side its base. Center this triangle, right side up, at the bottom of the backing strip. Its tip and the base midpoint should line up on the guideline. Stitch along the base of the triangle, joining it to the backing fabric ¼ in. from the edge (see illustration 1 on the facing page).

3 Next, lay one long contrasting strip face down along the right-hand side of the triangle, aligning the raw edges. The strip should just cover the triangle tip (see illustration 2 on the facing page). Using a ¼-in. seam allowance, stitch the strip in place. Begin stitching at the top of the triangle, and stitch to the edge of the muslin backing. Don't backstitch, since you don't need to secure your stitches.

4 Finger-press the strip back so that the right side of the fabric faces up, then trim the strip even with the backing fabric (see illustration 3 on the facing page). Hint: Don't trim before you finger-press or your side strip will not cover the backing.

5 Using the same technique just described, apply the left-hand strip. Be sure that the top of the strip barely covers the triangle tip. Again, stitch from the top to the base of the triangle in a ¼-in. seam (see illustration 4 on the facing page). Finger-press the strip back, and cut off the remainder of the strip even with the muslin backing, as shown in illustration 5 on the facing page.

6 As you did before, prepare your second triangle by pinch-marking the midpoint of its base. Using a pin point, mark this midpoint ¼ in. from the edge of the triangle's base, then place this triangle face down with its tip pointed downward. Place the pin point at the very tip of the exposed triangle, and align the tip of the triangle

By the Way

Fabric stores sell plastic specifically for making quilters' templates. However, you can cut thrifty templates from the transparent plastic lids of coffee cans and other household products. To do this, cut equilateral triangles in a variety of sizes, then mark their height with a permanent marker. Store them together in a see-through container.

with the guideline on the base fabric. After pinning in place, stitch down the triangle ¼ in. from its base (see illustration 6 at right). This line of stitching should be just one thread above the tip of the triangle to allow for turn of cloth, if you're very fussy.

7 Flip the triangle upward, and finger-press in place, aligning the tip with the guideline (see illustration 7 at right).

8 Finally, continue adding triangles and strips in this manner until you've reached the end of your backing fabric. Once you've framed the last triangle, add contrast strips until the muslin backing is completely covered (see illustration 8 at right).

Afghani piecing variations Here are some ways to vary the look of your Afghani strips.

- Construct the muslin strip on which the piecing is constructed in a different width. The strip can also be wider at one end, like a triangle with its top cut off. Simply trim the side strips to the backing as you construct the piecing.

- Using two solid colors for each of your triangles and strips, alternate them for an Amish-quilt effect.

- Choose a solid fabric for your triangles and a striped fabric for your contrast strips. Cut the 1½-in. strips from both the lengthwise and crosswise grains so you'll have both horizontal and vertical stripes. These can be randomly applied or alternately applied.

- For an elegant, subtle effect, use two different striped fabrics with similar scales and values for both triangles and strips.

- Experiment with color. Try colors you love with colors that you're not

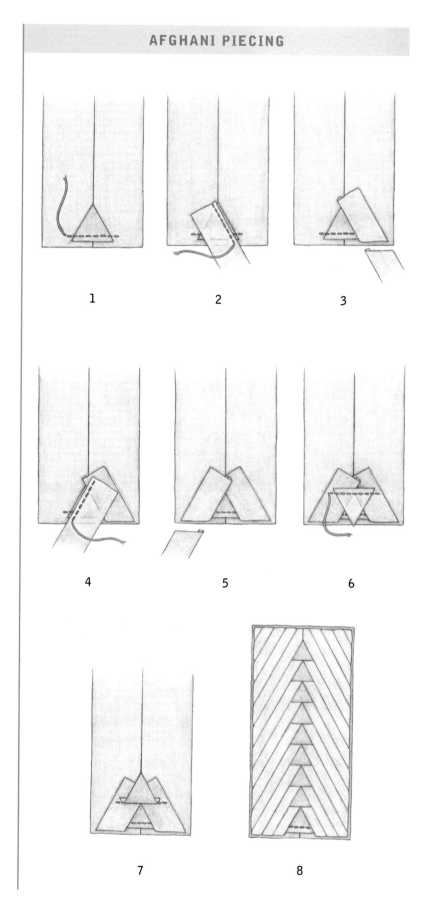

1

2

3

4

5

6

7

8

Sew two strips of fabric together to form triangles made up of both.

it so that each triangle is made up of two different fabrics (see the illustration at left).

- Take advantage of your clear triangle template. Center it over a motif in a print, then cut a triangle. Cut all subsequent triangles the same, or alternate two or more motifs. You can also make a series of triangles, each with a different related motif in its center. For example, feature leaves or geometric designs.

- Insert one or two unexpected triangles into a series of matching ones. They might be a printed fabric motif, a fabric you've painted or embroidered yourself, a fabric you've stamped, your initials and the date, or a piece of ribbon or flashy lamé.

Curved Afghani piecing While experimenting with Afghani piecing, I found that there were sometimes rewards for veering off the straight and narrow. This isn't a technique you can use on the center back of a lining, but I'm including it here because you need the previous information on doing traditional Afghani piecing before you can embark on this variation.

To make an arcing Afghani strip, cut your backing fabric in the shape of a gentle curve like the one shown in the photo on the facing page. Draw a center guideline as before, following the curve of the fabric.

You can cut all your triangles the same size. However, your framing strips for the outside edge of the curve must be cut ¼ in. to ½ in. wider than those used on the inside edge, depending on the angle of the curve. The sharper the curve, the wider you'll need to cut your strips. Use the same technique described on pp. 124–125 for sewing the strips and triangles in place.

You can make a short length of curved Afghani piecing go a long way on a gar-

so fond of. For a jolt of color sensation, use complementary colors (those that are opposite each other on the color wheel). Make your triangles and side strips from graduating colors of the rainbow—at full intensity or in paler tints. Use a monochromatic color scheme, also graduating the colors by value. Try using side strips that change from dark to light with the triangles within going from light to dark.

- Experiment with textures by using fabrics that contrast matte and shiny or smooth and bumpy.

- Experiment with shape. Shear off the tops of your triangles to make flat-topped quadrangles.

- Sew two long strips of fabric together and cut your triangles from

With just a little maneuvering, Afghani piecework can be coaxed into gentle curves. *(Photo by Grey Crawford.)*

ment if you cut it into sections, arrange the sections in a natural arc, and fill the areas between with fabric collage (see the illlustration at right).

MAKING PIECED MEDALLIONS

Since childhood, I've been fascinated by kaleidoscopes, and now I'm intrigued by the similarity of their designs to the designs of mandalas. Mandalas don't always have symmetrical or mirror images like those seen in kaleidoscopes, but their designs do usually appear within a circle or a square within a circle. Mandalas come to us from spiritual traditions around the world and are a symbol of healing and wholeness. They make inspiring subject matter for fiber art. The mandalas I've drawn over the years have been signposts indicating the direction of my spiritual and artistic journey.

Several years ago, I became aware of the exceptional kaleidoscope quilts that Paula Nadelstern was making. Occasionally I'm inspired to take on a small project that challenges my technical sewing skills just to prove to myself that, if I want to, I can still do precision sewing. During one of those moments, I decided to make a simple kaleidoscope quilt block, but because that was

GETTING THE MOST FROM A SHORT PIECE

Cut a short piece into sections, arrange them in an arc, then fill in the areas in between with collage.

A bead-embellished medallion is made up of wedges cut from a Liberty fabric that sported bands of design. *(Photo by Rosemary Eichorn.)*

are medallions made up of very complex pieced wedges. Simple medallions and complex kaleidoscopes can also be mandalas. You can name your circles whatever you want.

If you enjoy technically accurate sewing and want to learn how to make real kaleidoscopes with complex pieced wedges, I recommend that you get a copy of Paula's book. Making perfect kaleidoscope blocks requires patience and precision because each piece of the wedge must be cut exactly to size and each seam must match the rest. There's real satisfaction in the result of such accomplished sewing.

However, if you botch your first try at a perfect kaleidoscope or if you never aimed at perfection to begin with, who's to know this once you've slipped it into a collage that you've stitched and textured. If your points don't meet exactly in center, you can always embellish them. So I encourage even less-than-meticulous sewers to try at least one medallion.

To make your medallion, you'll need:

• A see-through ruler marked with angles

• A piece of 8½-in. by 11-in. plain white paper

• A pencil

• A piece of 8½-in. by 11-in. template plastic

• Craft scissors for cutting your template plastic

• About ½ yd. of fabric with bands of design

• A rotary cutter and cutting board

Making a striking medallion is based on about 20% sewing skill and 80% fabric selection. Imagine looking through a real kaleidoscope. If its bits of glass were all similar in size and color value, you'd soon be bored with the view. And if you sew together wedges of a fabric with a muted,

before Paula wrote her inspiring book, *Kaleidoscopes and Quilts,* I was on my own.

I divided a circle into 12 equal parts and came up with triangles with 30-degree angles. I made a template, cut 12 fabric wedges, and carefully sewed them together. I can't tell you how excited I was when I ended up with a flat medallion. Naturally, as I'm inclined to include my experiments and explorations in my collages, that medallion—and its offspring—ended up on my back. (The photo above shows a vest with one of these medallions.)

I'm using the word medallion to name a circular design made up of any number of identical, patterned wedges. Kaleidoscopes allover print, it will simply look from a distance like a solid circle of that fabric.

For a dramatic medallion, find a print with a bold design and strong contrasts. The design should be directional (meaning it has elements that have an up and down to them) and contain a variety of design elements. If you look at the photo on the facing page, you'll see concentric bands of designs. Each band is made up of a different design element—leaves, flowers, or arabesques. If the fabric had had only one allover design element—cabbage roses, for example—there'd be no variation in the wedges. So look for fabrics that have bands of designs in light and dark values.

Cutting wedges for medallions When cutting the pieces for a medallion, I prefer to use a homemade template rather than a commercial one because I'm easily distracted by ruler markings. Your template must be transparent because you'll be using it as a "finder" to identify 12 identical pieces of fabric. It's helpful if your template has a straight line bisecting its point and baseline.

1 To cut pieces for a 10-in. medallion, begin by drawing a 5-in. line lengthwise on your paper, making sure that it's 1 in. to 2 in. from the edge.

2 Using the 30-degree angle line on a see-through Omnigrid ruler, mark the angle for the other 5-in. leg of your triangle.

3 Complete your triangle by connecting the two legs to form a straight baseline. The first two sides can be any length you choose—as long as they're equal.

4 Next, add a ¼-in. seam allowance to each of the long sides of your triangle.

5 Trim the tip of the triangle ¼ in. beyond the point of the triangle.

6 Placing your template plastic over this pattern, use a fine-point permanent marking pen to precisely trace the pattern onto your template plastic. Trace the seamlines as well as the cutting lines.

7 Cut out your plastic template, making sure the template's edges are perfectly straight, then set it aside for a moment.

8 Next, use your paper pattern to make a viewing window. Cut out the triangle along the inside lines, which are the seamlines, rather than the cutting lines. This window will make it easier to isolate areas of fabric to make identical wedges.

9 Scoot your paper window template around on your fabric until you frame a wedge of fabric that contains the design elements you want repeated in your kaleidoscope.

10 To define the inside dimensions of your wedge, mark the three points of the triangle on the fabric. Then place your plastic template here, aligning the points of the template's seamlines with those marked on the fabric.

11 Use your rotary cutter to cut out the wedge, including its seam allowances. Mark enough of this fabric wedge's design lines on your template to serve as a placement guide.

12 Using these marks to place the template, cut out 11 more wedges that are identical to the first.

Sewing medallions Once you have all your pieces cut out, you can begin sewing them into your medallion.

1 With right sides together, carefully match the designs of two wedges along the long sides, and pin the seams.

2 Set your sewing machine's stitch length at 16 to 18 stitches per inch, then lower the needle by hand into the fabric exactly at the point where the seamlines intersect at the tips of the triangles.

3 Slowly take four or five tiny stitches, then reset the stitch length for normal stitching for the remainder of the seam. Don't add bulk at the tip by backstitching. Always sew from the triangles' tips to their bases.

4 Stitch all 12 wedges to complete the medallion. Each time you add a new wedge, manipulate the other seam allowances out of the way and start sewing at exactly the same point ¼ in. from the tip of the triangle.

5 When all the wedges have been stitched, press each seam to the side in the same direction. If you've been obsessively meticulous, you'll see those tiny points meeting perfectly at a flat center, like the blades on a camera's shutter. On the other hand, if your

A medallion is integrated into the collage design by covering some of its edges with motifs. *(Photo by Grey Crawford.)*

attitude has been more relaxed, you may have ended up with a hole or a small lump in the center. Somewhere you're sure to have exactly the right button or charm to embellish your collage at that point.

Now that you've made a simple, basic medallion, let go of your inhibitions the next time around. For example, you might alternate wedges in two contrasting fabrics—or throw in a single unmatched wedge. If you think your life lacks challenge, then use striped fabric—and be sure to match the stripes!

Incorporating medallions into collage
Your completed medallions can be used on either the outside or the lining side of a collaged garment. They can be incorporated into your collage in a number of ways so that they aren't just floating on top of the design. You can frame the medallion entirely with fabric collage to hide its raw edges, or you can use motifs and embellishment to cover just parts of it. You could also treat it like one big piece of collage fabric, with edges that appear and disappear like other motifs in your collage.

If you've made a fabulous medallion that you want to feature as star of the show, forget about integrating it into the larger picture—plunk it on the middle of your lining. You can leave the edges alone to fray naturally, or you can hide them under a narrow trim, couched-on flatlock beads, or heavy cord.

MAKING BARGELLO PIECING

Like many textile artists, I use techniques that have evolved from a background in traditional sewing and quilting. Not long after I began quilting, I realized that I was bored by the time I finished a couple of blocks of the same pattern. I would give up on my vision of a completed quilt and move on to a different block design or a new quilting technique. As a result, I never became an accomplished quilter, but my love of old quilts, their designs, and their techniques is as strong as ever.

Several years ago, I was intrigued by bargello quilt designs that were derived from the needlepoint technique of the same name. Bargello designs are characterized by undulating and zigzagging lines. I liked the way the values of the colors marched along in waves, creating repetition and movement over the surface of the cloth.

Examining them closer, I realized the movement was further enhanced by the gradual increase and decrease of the sizes of the tiny pieces of fabric that made up the bargello design. I couldn't resist making a sample of bargello quilting to satisfy my curiosity about the technique, and the result was a sizeable hunk of bargello piecing that I didn't know what to do with.

I decided to incorporate that sample into a lining. To extend a piece of lining fabric to make it wide enough for a vest, I used a 5-in. insert from the bargello sample. I liked the effect, especially when I added a bit of soft-edge appliqué at the bottom of the insert. Since then, I've made larger segments of bargello piecing and used them in lieu of plain fabric when making a collage.

Here's an easy way to do a sample that will teach you the basics of bargello piecing.

1 Select 10 fabrics that range in value from very light to very dark and arrange them in order according to their values.

2 Next, cut an on-grain strip, either crosswise or lengthwise, from each fabric. The strips should measure 2 in. wide and 22 in. long (about half the width of your fabric).

3 Keeping the strips in graduating color-value order, stitch them together using ¼-in. seams.

4 Press each seam toward the darker strip.

5 When you have stitched the last strip in place, sew its raw edge to the raw edge of the first strip to form a tube.

6 Press the tube flat, and align it with a line on your cutting board, making sure the tube is squared off.

7 Using a rotary cutter, slice 2-in. sections from the tube.

8 Next, use a seam ripper to open up the first tube between the fabrics of lightest and darkest values (see the left illustration on p. 132). Then open up each tube at the next value, moving down the value scale in succession. Keep the tubes in order as you open them.

9 Sew the new strips together with ¼-in. seams in the order in which you opened them. You'll see the values forming a pattern as you join the strips.

"Sunshine on My Shoulder": Bargello piecing is used in lieu of a solid piece of fabric to create the "sunshine" on this vest. *(Photo by Jack Deutsch.)*

Cutting the Tube

Cut off 2-in. sections with a rotary cutter and straight edge.

Use a seam ripper to open each slice.

The Finished Basic Bargello Sample

10 After all of the strips are joined, press the seams to one side. You've made a bargello sample with all of the movement cascading downward like a waterfall (see the illustration above right).

For a more advanced variation, graduate the slices cut from the tube by reducing the size of each successive one by ¼ in. Slice one will be 2 in., slice two will be 1¾ in., slice three will be 1½ in., and so forth. Make your narrowest slice 1 in. wide, then start making them gradually wider again (see the left illustration on the facing page). Keep these slices in order—they'll be sewn together in the order in which they were cut.

This technique can be expanded upon by making wider strips or more strips, varying the width of the strips, adding plain strips between the pieced strips, and so on. You've probably already figured out that by changing the order in which you open the tubes, you can change the direction of the pattern's movement. For instance, you can

start opening up tubes at the lightest value until you get to the darkest value, then reverse the order in which you open them until you get back to the lightest value again. This creates a big V shape, which is the traditional bargello design (see the right illustration on the facing page).

BOBBIN COUCHING

Couching means stitching a heavy thread in place with a lighter-weight thread. This is another technique that has been adapted from traditional hand-embroidery to machine-embroidery. When a heavy thread is placed in the bobbin, it is held in place by the lighter top thread so that the bobbin thread lies along the surface of the lining rather than being drawn up into the fabric. This quality gives you a wonderful opportunity to embellish the lining of your garment with designs that echo those of your collage.

Remember those aggravating metallic threads that frayed and broke when you tried to sew with them? Well, the bobbin is the place where all untamable threads go when they've shown themselves impossible to work with as top threads. Of course, well-behaved threads go on the bobbin, too, including many whose only sin is being too heavy or too wide.

Although you want to avoid using bobbin threads that are fuzzy, you have many options, including heavier metallics like Kreinik's cord, Madeira's Glamour, and YLI's Candlelight. Also consider using ribbon floss; thin silk or polyester ribbons; 1/16-in. and 1/8-in. satin ribbons; crochet yarns; novelty metallic yarns sold for use in loopers of sergers; fine chenilles; and other unusual imports found in stores that sell materials for making fishing lures.

Winding your bobbin When you use a heavy or novelty thread in your bobbin, never fill it more than three-fourths full. If your bobbin is accessible while it winds, you can use the bobbin winder's help.

1 Start by adjusting your machine for bobbin winding, and switch to half-speed if you have that option.

2 Secure one end of the thread on the bobbin by threading it through the bobbin's hole or by hand-winding it. Next, try winding the thread through the usual thread guides. I'm amazed at how often that works.

3 If you can't wind through the thread guides, cradle the ball of thread loosely in one palm, and let the thread pass slowly through the V of two fingers as the ball unwinds.

4 If the method in step 3 doesn't work, wind your bobbin by hand.

Adjusting your sewing machine When you use a heavy thread or ribbon in your bobbin, you must make some adjustments on your sewing machine. First, you must decrease the tension on the top thread so that it will penetrate to the bottom of your fabric sandwich. This is one time when you don't want your top and bobbin threads to meet in the middle of the stitched fabrics. A heavy bobbin thread should lie on the surface of the lower fabric and not be pulled up into it.

MAKING A MORE ADVANCED BARGELLO SAMPLE

Cutting the Tube

Cut off sections that are gradually smaller toward the middle of the tube.

The Finished Advanced Bargello Sample

1 To adjust the tension in the bobbin case, get out your manual, turn to the page on bobbin-tension adjustment, and identify the turn screw.

2 If you're using your only bobbin case, first use a permanent pen to mark the present alignment of the screw groove on the case. This will save you time when you want to readjust to standard tension.

3 Follow your manual's instructions to gradually loosen the tension until it is appropriate for whatever thread is on your bobbin. The thread should come smoothly out of the case but not without some tension.

"September Song":
Heavy metallic threads
used in the bobbin make
it possible to superim-
pose leaf outlines on
this vest's lining. *(Photo*
by Jack Deutsch.)

Second, you must adjust the tension of your bobbin case. (If your repairperson has told you never to fiddle with the bobbin tension, you either need a new repairperson or a new machine.) You might want to purchase a second bobbin case. It saves time to be able to switch quickly from one case that is always adjusted for standard threads to another that is always being readjusted. Use a dab of fingernail polish or an Identi-pen to mark your second bobbin case.

4 To test the tension, take hold of the thread end, let the bobbin dangle, then give it a quick upward jerk. If no more thread unwinds, the tension's still too tight. The tension is just right when a few inches unwind, then the bobbin comes to a halt in midair.

Sometimes if you're using an especially thick thread or ribbon in your bobbin, you need to bypass the tension spring altogether and poke the end of the thread up through the hole that's beside the tension mechanism in your bobbin case (see the illustration on the facing page).

Using novelty threads When you use novelty threads, ribbon, or ribbon floss in the bobbin and stitch with the collaged side up, you will, of course, be jazzing up the lining with outlines of the images from the collage. Once the collage motif pieces are all securely sewn down and outlined at their

Loosen upper thread
tension when sewing
with heavy thread in the
bobbin. Notice that the
top thread shows as a
tiny dot holding the
bobbin thread in place.
If you don't want the
top thread to show,
match it to the bobbin
thread. *(Photo by Jack*
Deutsch.)

outer edges, you can switch to a less dramatic thread in your bobbin such as rayon or metallic.

Then, still stitching from the right side of your garment, you can stitch meandering and echoing lines that will appear on the lining and that will integrate the novelty threads into the overall texture on the lining. This is especially effective on a plain fabric or on one that has a subtle allover pattern upon which the bobbin threads can dance.

For drama, try stitching the outline of a simple shape on the lining so that it appears in ribbon floss or another heavy novelty thread on the outside of your garment. You can do this in several ways:

- Sew a large motif on the lining before you sew it into the garment. After the lining is added to the garment, sew over the motif again with the lining on top, this time using a heavy novelty thread in the bobbin. The image of the motif will appear on the outside of the garment stitched in the novelty thread.

- Use a photocopier to enlarge a motif that you've used in your collage, then trace its outline and a few of its major design lines onto Solvy or another water-soluble stabilizer, and pin it to the lining. Create a design that can be outlined with a continuous stitch, rather than one that requires lifting and repositioning the needle. Using a heavy decorative thread in the bobbin and a regular sewing thread or rayon thread in the needle, stitch over the design.

- Trace or draw an original design on water-soluble stabilizer, and pin it to the lining. Stitch as described in the previous paragraph.

ADJUSTING THE BOBBIN CASE FOR THICK THREAD

The thread bypasses the tension mechanism.

Normal threading pattern

Adjust the tension screw.

One of the simplest methods for embellishing the inside of collaged garments, especially coats, jackets, and tunics, is to use two weights of decorative threads in the bobbin when doing the free-motion stitching.

I do this as a two-step process.

1 First, thread your machine's needle with a decorative rayon or metallic thread to embellish the outside of the collage. In your second bobbin case, use a heavy thread that will show up on the lining as an outline of the collage's motifs. Some of the thread I like to use are round metallic ones such as Kreinik Medium #16 or Fine #32 braids, YLI's Candlelight, and 1/16-in. silk ribbon.

2 Adjust the tension on your bobbin so that the thread flows easily from it without freely unwinding. You may also have to loosen the upper tension of your machine. The needle thread's tension must be loose enough to loop down around the bobbin's heavy thread, allowing the bobbin thread to lie flat against the lining.

3 With the outside of the garment facing up and using free-motion sewing, outline important motifs so that their shapes are defined by the heavy bobbin threads on the lining side of the garment. Don't cut the threads when sewing between motifs;

just continue sewing to adjacent figures and outlining them.

For the second step, do the following:

1 Switch to your regular bobbin case, and wind your bobbin with a lighter-weight decorative thread such as Sulky Sliver or another metallic or rayon thread.

2 Embellish the collaged portion of the garment with free-motion stitching, then use echo stitching or one of the other background fill stitches suggested on p. 104 to hold the lining and fashion-fabric layers together. This background stitching can be done with the same bobbin thread used on the collage or with one of a contrasting texture or color.

"Humble Origins": This linen lining was painted after the topstitching was completed. The bobbin threads form an outline that even novice painters can follow. (Photo by Jack Deutsch.)

The result is a beautifully textured lining that gets raves whether the garment is made to be reversible or not.

PAINTING THE LINING

Unless you're already an experienced fabric painter, the idea of painting on a finished garment may seem as daunting as climbing Half Dome at Yosemite National Park. Let me assure you, however, that the method I'm going to explain is more like painting in a coloring book than painting the Mona Lisa. Referring to the instructions in the previous section, think of the bobbin threads that outline the motifs as the lines in a coloring book that will show you where to paint.

Painting a garment's lining is best done after the garment's edges are finished but before the final laundering. When I'm planning to paint a lining, I add a capful of Synthropol to the first laundering's wash water to make sure that all of the textile's finishing resins and sizing are removed. Synthropol also helps keep the dye molecules of your collage fabrics from transferring to plain or light-colored linings. This step may not be necessary, but since I've had good results using it so far, I'm not going to push my luck.

Choosing a paint I use textile paints rather than dyes for this project because they are less complicated to work with. Dyes are watery and bleed unless you use a resist to contain them. Some require special steaming equipment to heat-set. Textile paints can be thinned with water to become very transparent, which will make them bleed like dyes. But when I want transparent colors for this project, I use extender or textile medium, which maintains the thick consistency of paint. For heat-setting, I use my household iron or my Elnapress. This is the one time I *do* break my rule and touch my collages with an iron. I count on the final laundering to restore the texture.

Lumiere metallic paints and Neopaque fabric paints are my favorites because they have lots of pigment particles. Lumiere is extraordinarily metallic. Both paints even cover dark colors because they are so opaque. They can be cleaned up with soap and water and can be heat-set with an iron or dryer. They produce fine detail, so they can be used for stamping, silk screening, and stenciling. As a bonus, they'll also work on most synthetics and blends in addition to natural fibers, which multiplies your lining choices. I've even used Lumiere to paint a leather purse. Got an old pair of leather tennies you want to jazz up?

I've also had success using Versatex, Createx, and Jacquard paints. In a pinch, I've even used acrylic paints from a craft store mixed with textile medium. You can't mix oil-based paints with water-based paints, but my concerns about toxicity—as well as my fondness for easy cleanups—make me steer clear of oil-based paints anyway. Most water-based textile paints claim to be non-toxic, but I am very cautious using any product that has pigments. I don't want surprises in the future, so I dedicate utensils, brushes, water containers, and mixing dishes to artwork and keep them separate from my kitchen utensils. I also avoid eating when I'm painting.

Purists probably don't mix products with different labels, but I've never claimed to be a purist. If a paint is water soluble, if I find it in my studio, and if it has the color, texture, and extending properties that I need, I use it regardless of its manufacturer. This may not work for painting garments that are going to go through the laundry every week, but the garments that I paint don't fall into that category. So far all of my painted fabrics have remained painted.

"All Creation Sings Her": Lumiere metallic paints were used to enhance the silk lining of this ensemble. (Photo by Jack Deutsch.)

If this is your first experience with textile painting, check what's available at your local art- or craft-supply store. You're more likely to experiment if you don't have to spend time and energy hunting down supplies or waiting for orders to be filled. Talk to salespeople to find out if any of them have had experience with textile design. Most artists enjoy sharing information

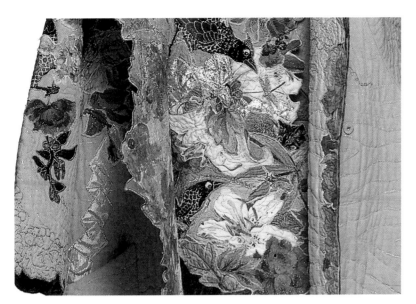

Dupioni silk accepts paint easily and makes a beautiful lining. *(Photo by Grey Crawford.)*

because they know you'll come back and share the results of your findings, too.

There are several fine books on painting textiles that address the qualities of the various brands of paints and the intricacies of textile painting (see Resources on p. 168). I've also found textile-supply catalogs to be one of my best resources for learning about textile paints. In addition, most mail-order companies have knowledgeable customer-service personnel who will listen to your questions and recommend products based on their experiences.

The painting method I'm describing here is easy and straightforward. Anyone can use this to successfully embellish her garments. Read the labels on your paints to learn specifics on using them, then relax, experiment, and have fun. I start experiments on a sample made from the same fabrics, underlining, and threads I've used in my garment.

Getting started Here are some suggestions to get you started on painting your lining. Start out with just a couple of brushes until you get a feel for the process. I like a No. 8 pointed round brush that's about half the size of my little finger, a ½-in. flat brush, and a No. 1 or No. 2 brush that's small enough for

painting details. Buy brushes in the mid-price range that are made for acrylic painting. Cheap craft brushes are frustrating because their bristles fall out, while expensive ones are overkill because fabric is hard on brushes, and they'll wear out faster than if you were painting on paper.

Since you'll be painting within the bobbin-thread outlines of motifs, use those same motif fabrics as models for your painting. Lay them near where you're working, and refer to them as you paint.

Use a soft lead pencil such as a Berol Draughting to lightly mark guidelines if you need more help than your stitched outlines provide. Water-soluble marking pens are made to disappear as soon as they get wet, but sometimes they don't completely wash out. I prefer the look of a leftover light pencil mark to that of a smudged blue mark left from a supposedly water-soluble pen.

1 Begin by creating a color palette that harmonizes with or contrasts with the colors of the more visible part of your garment. Although you may want to mix paints to match the colors of motifs on the outside of your garment, it's not necessary.

A soft lead Berol Draughting pencil is a good tool for adding guidelines for painting. *(Photo by Grey Crawford.)*

2 Try spritzing your lining ever so slightly with water before you start to paint. You may find this helps the paint go on more smoothly. The damper your fabric is to begin with, the more the paint will run and bleed. Having the paint run beyond the confines of the bobbin-thread outlines can be a wonderful effect.

3 Make your paints transparent by adding an extender following the manufacturer's suggestions. Using extender makes it possible to build up color gradually.

4 If you have a tendency to mix too many colors together until they become muddy, use a monochromatic color scheme. Take one color, and add varying amounts of white for lighter values. Add black or the color's complement (the color across the color wheel) for darker values.

5 Don't panic if your lining becomes fully saturated with water (which happens easily if you're thinning your paints with water instead of extender), and the pigments from your paints travel through the lining to the outside of your garment. This happens especially if you haven't used a muslin underlining. If this is the case, just dab on more areas of wet paint on the outside so that it looks intentional. Then when the painted area is dry, stitch over it with more free-motion stitching. It will look like you know what you're doing.

6 Clean your brushes out thoroughly when changing to a new color and again as soon as you've finished painting. You should use a mild soap and lukewarm water to remove the last traces of pigment from your brushes, then blot out the excess moisture, and lay the brushes flat to finish drying. If the phone rings while you're painting, ignore it. If you can't, drop your brush into a container of water or it may become history.

7 When heat-setting your paints, use a Teflon press cloth to protect your metallic threads. Heat-setting can take lots of time, so you may want to paint a selected area of your lining rather than the whole thing. Sometimes less is more.

The first lining that I painted gave me some surprising results. The lining was a medium-weight linen that had puckered a lot when it was washed. When I heat-set the paint, the color was more vivid on the peaks of the puckers than in the valleys because the peaks got more intense heat. Some of the pigment washed out of the valleys, and the result was a beautiful mottled effect. Now I can use that experience to intentionally get the same effect. The surprises I get every time I paint are what keep me interested in exploring this technique.

Painting onto a water-dampened fabric with textile paints that have been thinned with water creates a watercolor effect that may flow the paint beyond the confines of stitched or drawn lines. *(Photo by Grey Crawford.)*

8

Bringing Closure to the Task

By the time I've finished a collaged artwear garment, I've often used up so much time, energy, and physical resources in the project that my creative reserves are exhausted. I've made decisions about style, fabric, lining, and design. I've stitched, constructed, and stitched some more. Often I've made samples and explored new techniques. There have been so many decisions to make that I'm more than ready to finish the project and to move on to the next.

When I got to this point in my earlier designing days, my clever solution for creating a closure was doing nothing at all. I made "clutch coats" that had no buttons, vests that had no closures, and tunics that flapped in the wind.

Then one day I found a little back street in Santa Barbara, California, that was lined with Victorian homes turned into antique shops. Behind one of them was a great-

grandma with a cottage full of antique buttons. You'd think I'd never seen a button before! I walked out of that shop with a new enthusiasm for closures and a resolve to find ways to create suitable fasteners for my collaged garments.

In my quest for finding the right buttons for my collaged vests, I first fell in love with European metal buttons with little jet-steel pieces held on with rivets. They depict animals and plants like the ones I use on my collages. At bead shows, I found opulent dichroic glass buttons that were small works of art and that also mirrored the colors that I used in my vests. Their sparkle related to the dewy webs of metallic threads that traced across my collages. Along the way, I met Jean Keeshin, a talented designer of contemporary metal buttons. She crimps, textures, and layers metals in a way that makes her buttons natural exclamation points on collages.

(Photo opposite by Grey Crawford; photo above by Jack Deutsch.)

Buttons make a handsome addition to a studio's decor while they wait to become the perfect addition to artwear. *(Photo by Grey Crawford.)*

My appreciation of such special buttons hasn't made me a button snob. My buttons don't need a pedigree, so I'm perfectly happy with reproductions such as Czech pre-War glass buttons. I purchase some buttons just because they need an appreciative owner. The only limitation I put on my button buying is that I won't pay more than $20 for a button—well, hardly ever. A unique garment is worthy of the *right* closure at any price.

I'm gradually becoming a more discriminating collector, passing up the ones I know I won't use. I remind myself that cute theme buttons don't work on most of my garments. After all, those porcelain hot dog and mustard buttons I love so much have been in my drawer for years. On the other hand, if I come across a really great insect button, it will probably find a home in one of my imaginary gardens.

I've also become more realistic about the size of the buttons I buy. Small ones are lost on most of my garments, so I try not to buy ones that are smaller than 1 in. across unless I can use them purely as embellishments or can group them to make a statement. Since reading Lois Ericson's *Opening & Closing*, I've also been inspired to look for buckles, beads, and old jewelry parts that can be creative substitutes for buttons.

Never apologize for a collection of buttons and fasteners, even if you've had to claim freezer space for storage. I know from experience that it's much easier to find the absolutely perfect closure for a garment if I already own it. Last-minute combing of local stores without any luck and finally settling for a sort-of-okay fastener can undermine the effect of the best artwear.

Which Is the Right Button?

Because I don't have a blueprint for a garment when I begin designing, I often make a final closure decision as I'm finishing the project. To determine if a fastener really is perfect for a particular garment, I pin it where it will be used. Then I check out the effect from a distance as well as close up. This is much easier if you can shop your own button stash, but take your garment with you if you must make your selections away from your sewing room.

I like my closures to appear to grow from the garment's concept so they're not added on like a carnation corsage on a dinner jacket's lapel. When selecting a button or other fastener, consider the following points:

- Is its size compatible with the scale of the garment? Tiny buttons are likely to get lost on a long coat unless they're creatively grouped.

- Is its size compatible with where it's going to be located on the garment? A rather substantial button is needed if it stands alone on the overlap extension of an asymmetrical vest.

- Does its texture resemble that of the garment's fabric or its stitched surface textures? For instance, look for metal buttons with wrinkles to use on wrinkled collage surfaces.

- Does it mimic some aspect of the design of your garment? A leaf-shaped button will look at home on a tunic that sports flowers and leaves.

- Does it mimic a predominant fabric in your collage? A button with a checked pattern will look great on a collage featuring a checkerboard accent fabric.

Of course, the fastener you choose isn't going to match every one of these criteria. But the point is a fastener must relate to *some* element of the garment's design.

A well-designed closure is an integral part of a garment's overall design. This contemporary frog closure is paired with an antique brass button with steel jets. Kitty has her eye on those birds! *(Photo by Jack Deutsch.)*

Jazzy Closures

I'll probably never invent a new way of fastening garments, but it's fun to tweak the traditional way of making closures. Here are some fastener solutions I've adapted for my collaged garments, and they may also act as springboards for your creativity.

MAKING A COLLAGED BUTTONHOLE

Let's look at how you can create closures that are compatible with collage. The most obvious way to close a garment is by sewing a button on one side that fits through a slit buttonhole on the other side. Since my finishing techniques lack facings, a traditionally machine-stitched buttonhole will typically end up wavy-edged on a collaged garment unless I reinforce the buttonhole.

1 To reinforce the buttonhole and blend it into the collage, make two triangles about 1¼ in. high from a scrap of fabric, or use leftover edging triangles. Because these triangles will show on both sides of the garment, choose a fabric that will look good on each side.

The first side of a traditional buttonhole is encased in a 2-in. triangle topstitched in a forward and reverse pattern. *(Photo by Grey Crawford.)*

2 After machining a buttonhole the right size and cutting it open, slip one point of the first triangle through the slit and arrange it flat on the garment.

3 Working outward from the slit, free-motion stitch this point of the triangle in place.

4 Flip the garment over, and fold the rest of the triangle so that the triangle encases the buttonhole's slit (see the photo above).

5 Repeat these steps with the second triangle, encasing the opposite side of the buttonhole's slit. This produces a neat buttonhole that won't stretch out and that practically disappears into the collage around it. The reinforcing fabric doesn't have to be cut into triangular shapes, but as I said, I'm usually low on creative inspiration by the time I get this far.

MAKING A FROG FROM BIAS-COVERED CORD

For a more captivating closure, instead of a buttonhole I make a contemporary version of a frog to loop over a button. Rather than buy commercial cord, I make my own from a piece of thin (2mm) nylon drapery cord covered by a bias strip. Drapery cord makes a strong frog that won't shrink or stretch, and its scale is appropriate for clothing. The longer the cord is, the more intricate the design of the frog can be. The downside of using a long cord is that it takes longer to stitch the frog in place. Although this can be tedious if hand-stitching isn't your favorite diversion, I haven't yet figured out a way to do it by machine that satisfies me.

I usually make my frogs from an 18-in. cord but have used pieces as short as 10 in. and as long as 26 in. Here's how to make bias-covered cord. (Incidentally, this cord has lots of uses. I learned how to make it years ago from an article on sewing lingerie straps.)

1 Begin by cutting cording that is twice the desired finished length plus 3 in.

2 Cut a bias strip of fabric that is the desired finished length and 1¼ in. wide.

Bias-covered cord is loosely knotted and coiled to form a looped closure. The button is a doughnut-shaped disk held in place with a Chinese knot. *(Photo by Jack Deutsch.)*

18-in. bias strip — →   39-in. cord — →

1. With a bias strip folded around half of a cord, stitch the length of the strip 1/16 in. from the cord.

2. Holding the end of the cord that peeks out from the bias tube, ease the tube over the exposed half of the cord so that the tube is turned right side out.

3. The tube is now right side out with the seam allowance on the inside.

3 Next, attach a zipper foot to your sewing machine. Fold the bias strip around half the cord with right sides together, letting several inches of cord protrude from the bottom of the bias strip.

4 Starting where the end of the bias strip meets the middle of the cord, stitch across the cord and the strip several times so that the cord is securely attached to the strip. Stop about 3/8 in. from the strip's folded edge with your needle down.

5 Turn your work so you can stitch the seam down to the end of the cord as if you were making piping. As you stitch the length of the bias strip, angle your stitches toward the cord, creating a little "funnel" (see the top drawing in the illustration above). You should stitch the length of bias strip about 1/16 in. from the cord. If you stitch too close to the cord, there won't be enough room for the seam allowance inside the bias tube when the cord is turned.

6 Trim the seam allowance to 1/8 in.

7 Take hold of the short end of the cord that peeks out from inside the bias tube. Pulling on the cord, ease the bias tube over the long exposed half of the cord so that you are turning it right side out and covering this second half of the cord (see the center and bottom drawings in the illustration above). The seam allowance is now on the inside of the bias tube.

8 Cut off the excess cord.

By the Way

After you've turned a bias tube over a cord as described above, you can cut the stitches that secure the bias strip to the middle of the cord and pull the entire cord from the bias tube. This gives you a tiny flexible bias tube that can be used like a heavy decorative yarn to embellish the surfaces of artwear, quilts, and garments. You can secure it with hidden hand-stitches, or you can couch it in place by hand or machine. Larger bias tubes can be created by sewing wider bias strips over larger cording.

Making the Button Loop

Pin cording for a button loop in place, and try slipping it over your button before sewing the cord in place.

Sewing Down the Button Loop

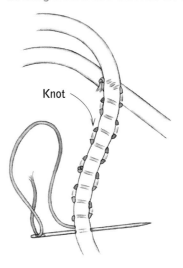

Knot

Hand-sew tiny ladder stitches on the underside of the cording to hold it in place. Forming knots every 1 in. to 2 in. will make repairs easier should a stitch break due to wear and tear.

A bias-covered cord, about 18 in. long, is used to design a free-formed frog that knots and bends at the point of closure on a collaged vest. *(Photo by Jack Deutsch.)*

To fashion a frog fastener, you must first empty both ends of the bias-covered tube so that you can clean-finish these ends. Do this by pushing back the tube at both ends and snipping off about ½ in. of the drapery cord. Use an awl or T-pin to poke the raw ends back inside the tube, then hand-stitch the tube closed. Alternatives to clean-finishing the ends are to tie a knot close to each end of the cord and let the raw ends fray or to hide the raw ends under the frog as you shape it.

You should design your frog closure right on the front of the garment. First, place the cord's midpoint at the edge of the garment where it is to loop over the button. Fashion a loop that will accommodate your button, then pin it in place so that the loop is just beyond the cord at the edge of your garment (see the illustration above left). This will make it accessible from both sides of your reversible garment.

Next, start looping the cord like the tendrils on a pumpkin vine. Use a section of cord to make a large, loose knot, then weave the end of the cord in and out of the knot. When you like the effect, pin the cord in place, and arrange the next length of it.

When your frog is completely pinned down, check how it looks with the button. Try on the garment, and pin your button so that it is in the right place for the frog to loop over it. Fasten your garment, then stand back to look at it. You may want to make adjustments before you stitch it in place.

When sewing on the frog, use a strong thread. I use quilting thread and run it through beeswax before I stitch. Begin by stitching one end of the button loop in place with tiny stitches. Then do a ladder stitch, taking tiny stitches to attach the lower sides of the cord to the garment (see the illustration above right). Knot the thread

1. Form loop A.

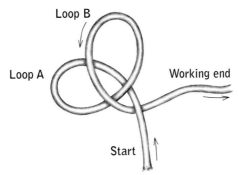

2. Holding loop A between the thumb and forefinger of your left hand, form loop B with your right.

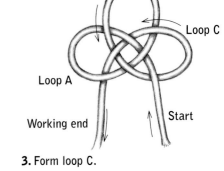

3. Form loop C.

4. To make a frog, pull the outer loops of the knot tight, leaving the center loop large enough to fit over a button.

5. To make a ball button, pull all of the loops tight and bind the two ends together .

every 1 in. to 2 in. of cording so that if the stitching does break later on, the whole frog won't pull off.

MAKING A FROG AND BALL BUTTON FROM BIAS-COVERED CORD

A ball button made from bias-covered cord is a good stepping-off place for creating your own one-of-a-kind buttons. To make a frog and ball button, start by making an 18-in. length of bias-covered cord following the instructions in the previous section. Then follow the first three illustrations above, holding the loops between the thumb and forefinger of your left hand and manipulating the working end of the cord with your right hand.

To form a simple frog closure, pull on the starting and working ends of the cord, tightening loops A and C and leaving loop B as the frog to loop over a button or other fastener (see the fourth illustration above). Loop B can be made smaller or larger by manipulating loops A and C. The starting and working ends can be cut short and have their raw edges hidden under a frog, or they can be looped in a symmetrical design to create a frog

A ball button is really a Chinese knot made by starting exactly as you did to make a frog. But instead of tightening the ends of the cord, pull on the cord where it forms loop B to tighten that loop first. Then pull the ends of the cord to tighten the outer two loops to create the knot (see the fifth illustration above). When using drapery

Once you've mastered the technique of making Chinese knotted balls, you'll discover many new ways to include them in your artwear projects.

• Pull two small Chinese knots through large holes in a button to hold the button in place instead of sewing it on in the usual way.

• Slip one or several tiny, stitched-together Chinese knots through the central hole in any doughnut-shaped disk or other object with a large hole, such as a brass washer or shell, to create a fastener. I've even found rusty washers lying along the

roadside that could be given a coat of polyurethane and used with Chinese knots to make uncommon fasteners. You can wrap the washer with fine wires, then use it alone or string it with seed beads. Finish off the back side by gluing on a piece of ultrasuede cut to fit.

• Cover three or more lengths of drapery cord or cover heavy, twisted cotton cord from the home decoration section of your fabric store to make a more substantial knot. This knot can become a button by itself when you wrap the cord ends with heavy buttonhole thread to form a shank.

• Group several Chinese ball buttons to work as one button on one side of your garment. Instead of cutting off the long cords, use them to form graceful knots and tendrils. Then create a lavish frog on the other side to loop over the ball buttons.

• Consider substituting a wonderful bead or a small button for the Chinese ball buttons in any of the above ideas. Bead stores, sewing shows, and catalogs provide not only conventional round beads but also beads shaped like bees, bats, bananas, and bells.

cord, this creates a tiny knot that's hardly large enough to be a button for the garments I create. See the sidebar on p. 148 for some of its possibilities.

Care of Special Buttons

Sewing on the perfect button is the last thing I do when I'm making artwear. It's my amen in the ritual act of creation and signifies my readiness to introduce my work to the world. Unless I dump salsa down the front side of a light-colored vest, it will probably be a long time before it needs laundering again. But even into the life of artwear, a little rain must sometimes fall, so here's how Stephanie Krenzin from the Button Shoppe (see Resources on p. 168) suggests we protect our little beauties from damage in the washing machine and dryer. (Remember, we never dry-clean a collage.)

In general, buttons of natural products such as horn, antler, bone, shell, tagua nut,

and stone can be gently washed. This is true of buttons made from glass, metal, and plastic as well. However, even the most durable buttons of metal and plastic do not hold up well to bleach, harsh detergents, or hours of soaking in water.

Avoid the dryer as much as possible and never overdry. The high heat and tumbling action of the dryer weaken the structure of buttons and lead to early discoloration, scratches, and breakage. Wash polymer clay buttons such as those made from Fimo and Sculpey in cool water only, and never put them in a dryer.

Buttons can be easily cushioned during the washing process in several ways. An old trick used by dry cleaners is to protect buttons in a cushioning ball of heavy-duty foil. I never learned to trust that the foil will stay on, so I prefer making reusable button protectors with extra-wide hook-and-loop tape.

To use this method, cut both sides of the hook-and-loop tape larger than the buttons they'll protect, and round the corners so they won't catch on other fabrics. The hook side of the tape is used as the bottom of the protector. Slit the bottom so that the button or thread shank can be positioned in the middle with the hooks facing up. The loop side of the tape goes over the button's face to form a neat protector sandwich.

Another of Stephanie's worthwhile suggestions is to customize your garment to make the buttons removable. This is an especially good technique for reversible garments or for valuable or fragile old buttons that may not like getting their feet wet. To do this, choose a second set of flat buttons that match the fabric, and attach them to the "show" button in a cuff-link fashion, making sure you leave a shank between the two that will accommodate the double thickness of the garment.

Add a second set of buttonholes the size of the "invisible" button where you would normally attach the buttons. Button the invisible backing button through this second set of buttonholes. This design feature has the additional benefit of allowing you to change your buttons or to be able to use a really special button on another garment.

Snappy Closures

An alternative to a button closure is a large snap. I plan some coats and jackets to be worn open over a coordinating outfit, but I like having the option of buttoning up against the elements. Sometimes a button closure interferes with the collage design on the outside of a garment, and a large snap or two will solve the closure dilemma. Dritz makes a ½-in. snap that's covered in white, black, or beige fabric that's strong enough to keep a coat or jacket closed. I like the convenience of buying a snap that's already covered, but the limited colors don't make a very inspired note on which to finish an otherwise fabulous garment.

If you want to color a snap, this is the time to bring out your fabric marking pens.

1 Start by choosing a color that either matches or contrasts with your garment, depending on how much of a statement you want your snap to make. You can mix several colors to match a garment perfectly, or you can use two or more colors to make a snappy statement.

2 Color the snap before you sew it on the garment so you can get the pigment on the edges and the undersides of the snap as well as on its face.

3 When you sew on the snap, consider using perle cotton in a contrasting color if you'd like to draw attention to your closure.

To further dress up a snap, you can add beads in a ring around the female part as I have done with the snap shown in the photo above. Make sure you use tiny seed beads that don't come above the top surface

Tiny seed beads adorn the large covered snaps used to close this coat. The receptor part of the snap is given prominence by being mounted on a tiny 9-patch block. (Photo by Grey Crawford.)

ADDING BEADING

Sew a backstitch through every other bead, and make a knot after every four beads to keep them securely in place.

"A Designer's Trip to Hong Kong": The tasseled closure on this tunic is based on the principle of envelope closures that use a strong string and two little cardboard disks. In this case, the disks are replaced by star-shaped buttons. *(Photo by Jack Deutsch.)*

of the snap or else the snap won't close. To do the beading, choose a beading needle and Silamide (see Resources on p. 168) or another strong beading thread, then refer to the illustration on p. 149. If you're cautious and like doing a job just once, knot your beading thread after every four beads have been sewn in place.

In the photo on p. 149, you'll see a tiny 9-patch, duplicating a traditional quilters' block, appliquéd in place before the snap and beading were added. Use this idea as a jumping-off place for more fantastic ways to use snaps to close your artwear. Each snap has the potential to be a mini work of art.

Manila-Envelope Closures

Inspirations for creative closures can come in the most unexpected places—an old-fashioned envelope used for sending a stack of papers through the mail, for instance. Remember the kind that had a little cardboard disk attached to the flap and another to the body of the envelope with a stiff string to wrap the two together? The 1998 *Threads* magazine designer challenge included the task of creating an "unusual closure" for a garment. I used the envelope-fastener principle for my tunic shown in the photo above. Here is how you can use this method.

1 First, attach buttons to both sides of each of the fronts of a reversible garment. These buttons don't have to be exactly the same size, but they should be close.

2 Make an 18-in. plied cord following the directions on pp. 144-145. I used threads unraveled from my tunic's silk suiting fabric and coordinating metallic threads.

3 Next, make three tassels from all of these threads, each 2½ in. to 3 in. long, to incorporate into the closure. You can adjust the measurements of the cord and tassels or other embellishments to suit your garment and its proportions.

4 Form a loop 6 in. from one end of the cord, and wrap it with a strong thread so that the loop will fit over one of the buttons.

5 To close the garment, tie the two cords together to form a second loop to fit over the button on the opposite front of the garment.

6 Finally, attach tassels. I attached three tassels, one to each end of the plied cord and one to a knot I added for texture to one length of the cord.

When I don't fasten the tunic, the tasseled cord hangs from one of the buttons like a piece of jewelry. When I reverse my tunic, the looped cord easily becomes the closure for that side.

Brass-Hasp Closures

A trip to the hardware store can be a creative excursion if you're thinking artwear instead of paint and nails. My stash includes a variety of rubber and brass washers and O-rings, brass screen mesh and cotter pins, and several brass hasps.

A ⅝-in. by 1⅞-in. decorative hasp was the inspiration for the closure shown in the photo below. The "loop" side of the fastener is sewn on the left side of the duster where a button would be located if this were a traditional closure. The single holes on either side of the loop provide opportunities for unusual sewing details.

1 To make a brass-hasp closure like mine, make an organic pattern of threads covered with free-motion zigzag stitching. Do this by using water-soluble stabilizer and a weblike base of threads pulled from torn cotton strips (see the right photo below).

2 Attach the threads to the flat side of the hasp by stitching through the holes intended for nails.

3 Next, machine a buttonhole the length of the slot in the flat side of the hasp on the right front of the garment, then hand-stitch the hasp in place, aligning the slot and the buttonhole.

4 Add the final component of this fanciful closure, which is a 12-in. covered or plied cord that fits through the loop of the hasp to hold the two sides of the garment together. To do this, stitch the middle of the cord near the slotted side of the hasp. The tip of one end of the cord slips through the loop of the hasp, and the two ends of the cord are tied to hold the whole thing together. A narrow drop bead, a cotter pin, or a slender piece of bone affixed to the end of the cord makes it easy to slip through the hasp's loop.

A search through the hardware store resulted in finding a brass hasp, which became the inspiration for this unusual closure. *(Photo by Jack Deutsch.)*

"Sunshine on My Shoulder": This duster's unique closure echoes the wispy vines and tendrils that embellish the collage. *(Photo by Jack Deutsch.)*

9

Little Extras Mean a Lot

What makes a collaged garment so much fun to work on is that just about anything you learned to do somewhere else can be worked into it. At different times and for different reasons, I learned to make prairie points and tassels, to make plied cords on my sewing machine, and to apply shisha mirrors and other flat disks by machine. And now all of them have showed up in my garments. So I'm passing on these techniques as additional ones you might like to use to embellish your collages.

Adding Prairie Points

Prairie points are the saw-toothed triangles that appear on the garment shown in the photo on p. 154. They're often used to edge baby quilts and are sometimes used singly to embellish garments. I'm going to describe how you can make bands of equally spaced prairie points like I use on some of my garments. If you're a traditional quilter,

you'll find this technique is an unbelievably easy alternative to making hundreds of points one by one and then stitching them together in an unbroken string. It's also almost impossible to space the points evenly when they're sewn together one by one. Using this method, you'll make them from a single long strip of fabric or two strips sewn together and treated as one.

Although prairie points look complicated, they're easier to make than a child's paper hat. Once you understand how to make just one prairie point, you'll have no trouble making a continuous band of them. For your practice activities, you'll work with paper because it's easier to fold when learning the technique and because the paper samples are convenient to keep as reminders of what you've learned. To make your samples, you'll need paper-cutting scissors and four photocopies of the illustration on p. 154 enlarged 200%.

There are two traditional ways to fold fabric to make prairie points. If you're not

(Photo opposite by Grey Crawford; photo above by Jack Deutsch.)

A band of tie-silk prairie points, slipped under the edges of collaged motifs, adds subtle texture. Their tips have been machine-tacked in place. *(Photo by Jack Deutsch.)*

familiar with them, go through the following square-folding process to learn them both.

First, you'll need to cut out one each of the squares labeled "Tent Prairie Point" and "Biting Prairie Point." I'll get to the reason for those names later. From now on, the patterned side of the paper will be called the "right" side, and the blank side will be called the "wrong" side. They are the equivalents of the right and wrong sides of fabric—if you still believe in such things.

MAKING TENT-TYPE PRAIRIE POINTS

I gave tent prairie points their name because the place where their folds meet in the middle reminds me of the opening of an old-fashioned tent.

1 To make a tent prairie point, first fold your square in half along the center foldline (A to B) so that the wrong side is inside.

2 Fold along the second set of foldlines (D to C and E to C). The points labeled A and B should meet at the central point F (see the top left illustration on the facing page). You've made a little prairie point that looks like a tent.

MAKING BITING-TYPE PRAIRIE POINTS

Biting prairie points are a snap to create with just two simple folds.

1 To make a biting prairie point, fold your square along the diagonal from point A to B, wrong side inward.

2 Fold along the second foldline (C to D) so that points A and B meet (see the center left illustration on the facing page).

3 Make a second biter prairie point. You'll notice a useful characteristic of this

PRAIRIE POINT PRACTICE SAMPLES

Tent Prairie Point

A — C — B

D   F   E

Biting Prairie Point

C ⋯⋯⋯⋯ B

D

A

Cut

Cut

Cut

Cut

Cut

Cut

MAKING BASIC PRAIRIE POINTS

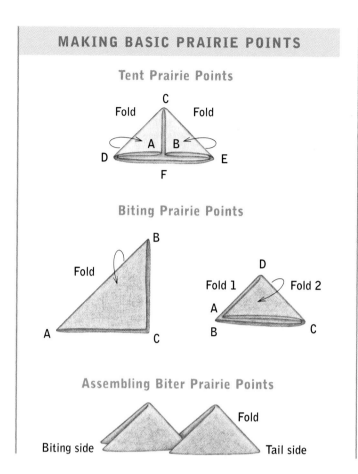

Tent Prairie Points

Biting Prairie Points

Assembling Biter Prairie Points

MAKING CONTINUOUS-STRIP PRAIRIE POINTS

Step 1

Step 2

Step 3

type of prairie point: You can take your second biter and insert its folded tail side into the open slot of the first biter (see the bottom illustration above left). Now you know how this prairie point got its name. Using biters slotted into one another gives you a smooth finish on both sides of your edging.

USING THE CONTINUOUS-STRIP METHOD

By using the continuous-strip technique, you can make numerous, equally spaced prairie points. For each of the following four variations, you'll need one cut-out experiment strip with the cuts made to the center foldline as indicated.

Variation 1: Using the tent This is the first of two variations you can try that uses tent prairie points.

1 Begin by laying the strip with its wrong side facing up. On both sides of the strip, fold each square in half toward the centerline as shown in the top illustration above right.

2 Next, working on one side only, make your second set of folds to create tents (see the center illustration above right). Notice that you are folding raw edges toward the raw edge already lying on the centerline.

3 Flip the strip over, then make your second set of folds on the remaining squares as shown in the bottom illustration above right. This time you are not folding raw edges toward a raw edge.

THE COMPLETED CONTINUOUS-STRIP PRAIRIE POINTS

4 Now simply fold the paper along the centerline. All of your tent flaps are facing the same way (see the illustration above).

Variation 2: Using the tent In this variation, you'll use a spiraling-fold technique to produce an alternating pattern of overlapping points. **Follow steps 1 through 3 of variation 1.**

4 Hold the strip up before you so that the topmost triangle is in your left hand and the smooth sides of the right-hand triangles all face toward you. You'll see that the left-hand triangles have their folded sides facing you (see the illustration below left).

5 Next, fold the uppermost right-hand triangle back toward the left along the center foldline. As you do this, the lower

triangles will automatically swing around (see the illustration below right). You'll see the smooth faces of the triangles on the right and the folded faces of the triangles on the left.

6 Again, fold the uppermost right-hand triangle toward the left and continue to do so until all the right-hand triangles are folded flat upon the left-hand ones as shown in the top illustration on the facing page.

Variation 3: Using biters This variation makes a traditional saw-tooth strip that is a popular edging for baby quilts. It's a much easier method than making individual prairie points and then sewing them together.

1 Place the strip right-side down. Working along one side at a time, fold each square diagonally to make a "Christmas tree." You'll be folding the topmost raw edge of each square toward the centerline as shown in the center left illustration on the facing page.

2 Next, make your second fold on each triangle, this time folding upward. When you have finished, all the raw edges of the triangles will be lying along the cen-

SPIRALING-FOLD TENT PRAIRIE POINTS

Step 1

To use this alternative continuous-strip method, hold the strip so the smooth sides of the right-hand triangles face you.

Step 2

Begin at the top to fold the prairie points into place one at a time.

terline (see the center right illustration at right).

3 Once again, fold along the centerline in either direction as you did for variation 1. The resulting points will look like the ones shown in the top illustration on the facing page, the only difference being that the front and reverse sides will both be smooth.

Variation 4: Using biters In this variation, take advantage of the biter's capacity to let you slot one triangle inside the following one. To do so, you can use a spiraling-fold technique similar to the one you used to make variation 2. **Follow steps 1 and 2 of variation 3.**

3 Hold the strip so that the topmost triangle is on your left and the open, biting edge faces upward. You'll notice that the side of the strip that faces you is the one with the raw edges lined up along the centerline.

4 Next, fold the topmost left-hand triangle forward toward the right-hand triangle. Instead of laying the left-hand triangle flat against the right-hand triangle, open the right-hand triangle up so that it wraps around and bites the tail of the left-hand one (see the bottom left illustration at right).

5 Fold the third triangle toward the right in front of the second triangle, then open its biting end to wrap around the second triangle.

6 Finish by folding every other triangle behind, instead of in front of, the right-hand triangles. You'll notice that you're always folding toward the line of raw edges. When you're done, the points will look like the ones shown in the bottom right illustration at right). Each tail will be bitten by the point that follows it.

OVERLAPPING THE TENT PRAIRIE POINTS

MAKING BITERS WITH A CONTINUOUS STRIP

Step 1

Step 2

Fold each square diagonally.

Fold the outermost point of each triangle upward.

SPIRALING-FOLD BITER PRAIRIE POINTS

Step 1

Open up each triangle as it is folded into place so that it bites the tail of the triangle above it.

Step 2

The biter prairie points are folded into place.

The tips of these tent-type prairie points are embellished with beads and a charm, which are added after the final laundering. Hand-laundering and air-drying are recommended after beaded details are attached. *(Photo by Grey Crawford.)*

MAKING PRAIRIE POINTS IN FABRIC

Once you've made these paper models, you'll find it easier to make the prairie points in fabric, and you'll have begun imagining how you can use them and vary them. Clearly, the strip doesn't need to be a solid piece of fabric. The centerline can be the seamline of two contrasting strips or of the same fabric with one side used wrong-side out. Here are some pointers for working with fabric.

- Use heavy-duty spray starch to spray and press your strips of fabric on both sides before you begin forming prairie points. You could also use a commercial fabric stiffener such as PerfectSew. The more paperlike your fabric is, the easier it will be to work with. The stiffening product will wash out in the laundry.

- Once you've cut your strips of fabric and marked and cut the squares, take your work to your ironing board. Work assembly-line style by pressing each of the folds with your iron once you've finger-pressed a series of them.

- The length of your completed chain of points will correspond to the length of your strip of fabric. To figure how wide to cut the strip, decide how high you want your prairie points to be from tip to base, not including the seam allowance if they will be inserted into a seam. Then, if you are using only one

fabric, multiply that number by four and add ½ in. That ½ in. will become a ¼-in. seam allowance once you have folded the fabric along the centerline.

- If you are using two different fabrics so that the prairie points will alternate in pattern, the width of each strip should equal two times the height of the prairie points plus ½ in. (¼-in. allowance for joining your two strips plus ¼ in. for the final seam allowance). To sew the two strips together, overlap their long sides ¼ in., and stitch with a zigzag or serpentine stitch. You could also eliminate the ¼-in. allowance for joining the strips, and simply butt the two long edges and stitch with a serpentine stitch.

- You can use any type of marker to indicate your cutting lines. You'll be marking off your strip into squares, the sides of which should equal the distance halfway across the strip. For example, if you want 1-in. triangles, cut a strip 4½ in. across, and mark its centerline 2¼ in. from either long edge. Mark your cutting lines 2¼ in. apart, then indicate all of the cutting lines along one side of the strip using a right angle to mark them. Then go back, find the midpoints of your first row of squares, and use those to mark the cutting lines on the opposite side of the strip.

- If you work like I do, you don't really care what the actual height of your prairie points is. You just want them to look right. In that case, you may prefer my renegade method to the one described above, with all of its precise measurements. I typically use two different fabrics so my points alternate in pattern or color.

First, I cut two long strips of fabric each of which look a little more than double the height that I want my finished prairie points to be. I butt the strips and sew them together with a serpentine stitch, then I measure the distance from that butted centerline to one of the long edges. That's the measurement I use to make my squares. I follow one of the folding techniques discussed previously to finish my prairie points.

- When you use prairie points in your collage, stitch them down near the center fold. They don't have to be laid out in the straight lines you normally see on the edges of quilts or pillows because a continuous band of them is so flexible that it can meander through your collage. You could also arrange short lengths of them so they seem to disappear and reappear among the motifs on your collage.

- You can hide the prairie points' raw edges under fabrics in your collage, or you can cover them with ribbon, braid, couched cords, or heavy decorative stitching. When laundered, the little points tend to become unruly, so I use bead trims or machine-stitched motifs at the tips to anchor them to the background and help keep them under control.

Making Plied Cords

This easy method for making cords is certain to be a favorite of anyone in love with fibers, fabrics, and textures. Handmade cords are perfect as hanging cords for tassels and other charms, for making button loops and frogs, or for couching onto a collage with a long zigzag, blind-hem, or other open decorative stitch. I'll describe the basic method first, then pass on some tips for making unusual, eye-catching cords for all kinds of sewing and art projects.

For practice, all you'll need are the following materials:

- A sewing machine with an exposed bobbin winder

KNOTTING CORDS TO A BOBBIN

- An empty bobbin
- Three 1½-yd. strands of yarn or cord such as #8 pearl cotton or Kreinik fine braid #8

You are going to attach one end of each of the three strands to the top of the bobbin and let the spin of the bobbin twist the strands together. There are a couple of ways in which you can attach the strands so that they hold fast to the spinning bobbin.

If your bobbin has a hole in the rim that's large enough to accept the cords, thread them through the hole and tie a knot to keep the threads from slipping out (see the illustration above).

If your machine uses plastic bobbins, you may want to enlarge the hole in one of them to accommodate slightly thicker cords and set it aside just for this use.

If your cords are too bulky to fit through the hole in your bobbin, tie a strong thread, such as buttonhole thread or dental floss, securely around the core of your bobbin, and thread its ends through a hole in your bobbin from the inside out. Clip these ends about 3 in. long, then tie the cords to them.

1 To begin making plied cords, engage your machine's bobbin-winding feature, and securely hold the free ends of the cords in one hand to keep them taut.

2 As you operate the machine, let the spinning bobbin twist the cords together. Since the cords tend to twist close to the machine, run the fingers of your free hand

- The finished cord will end up more than twice as thick as the cords you start out with. To get an idea of what your finished cord will look like, twist a 4-in. length of the candidate cords between the fingers of both hands, and let them twist back on themselves.

- Each cord you use should be three times the finished length you desire. I typically don't bother with measurements. I just tie the cords to my bobbin, then unreel them until the ends are as far from the machine as I can hold them with one hand and still be able to reach the machine's bobbin winder with the other. If the resulting cord is longer than you need, make two knots close together and cut

between them. Save the remaining cord for couching onto a collage, for making a frog to fasten a garment, or for tying a special gift. You'll find lots of uses for these sumptuous cords.

- Don't be afraid of color. Using three or four cords of closely related colors will produce a subtle effect. Throwing in an unexpected color and texture such as a fine metallic thread that's the complement of a predominant color will add character and pizzazz to your cord.

- Contrasting textures can be stunning when twisted together. Picture shiny Sliver threads plied with chenille, bouclé, and string.

- Two or more plied cords can be couched together side-by-side or loosely twisted together and stitched down. Use a zigzag stitch width setting of 2 and a length setting of 2½ and use a bulky overlock foot or other foot with a deep groove on the bottom. You can try using the blind-hem stitch for a different effect. Thread the machine's needle and bobbin with any thread that matches one of the cord's colors.

- Twist a plied cord loosely with a narrow bias-cut silk ribbon or with cords formed from narrow slices of fabric, then zigzag the cords together.

up the cords from the bobbin toward the top. This will move the twists upward.

3 Release the tension on the cords a bit to see if they're twisted enough. They are if they start twisting back on themselves, making a six-strand cord.

4 To take advantage of this characteristic, hold the midpoint of the double-strand cord in your free hand, and slowly release the tension on the cord. The cord will continue to twist back on itself so that the whole of it becomes a six-strand cord.

5 If you want to attach a bead, tassel, or other trinket to one end of a twisted cord, thread it onto the cord while still holding it taut. Put the bead in the middle of the cord, then release the tension. The bead will be held in place by the twisted cord.

6 Take the bobbin off the winding spindle, and cut it free.

7 Finally, tie an overhand knot at the cut end of the cord to keep it from untwisting.

Not everyone has a bobbin-winding mechanism that will accomplish this task. However, you can also twist cords by tying one end to a door knob and the other to a beater of a hand-held eggbeater. You can also buy a commercial cord winder that works on the eggbeater principle. Any of these will provide you with the means to do some serious long-cord twisting.

If you want just a short length of cord for hanging a little tassel, you can twist it by hand, using a little ingenuity. A safety pin will hold one end of your cords securely to your pant leg or other convenient spot, then you can twist the other end with your free hands. Another way is to lower the presser foot of your sewing machine on the knotted end of a length of cords to hold them in place while you twist them from the other end. Or if you're a gadget person, you can buy one of those clever "third hands."

Adding Tassels

I find tassels a totally irresistible embellishment. In *Tassels, The Fanciful Embellishment,* Nancy Welch calls them "the exclamation point of a textile sentence."

Historically, tassels have significance in many cultures. They add power to a shaman's magic, and according to Jewish tradition, the ones on a prayer shawl are a reminder to obey God's commandments. One of my favorite tassel metaphors is that the individual strands of a tassel represent all people who are brought together as one by the wrapping at the neck of the tassel.

My earliest tassel-making experience was creating an octopus from many long strands of yarn bound together over a cotton-stuffed head. The strands were divided into eight parts, and each part was braided to form a tentacle tied with a bright bow. I think that's where I learned the nifty dental floss trick described here that I use when I make quick and uncomplicated tassels.

To make a trial tassel, you'll need:

- Fine yarns, cords, strings, ribbons, or threads for the skirt
- A strong, smooth cord for wrapping the neck
- A decorative cord for hanging (a good use for the plied cord you just made)
- A 10-in. length of dental floss
- A sturdy piece of cardboard
- Scissors to cut the threads and the cardboard
- Beads or charms for embellishing, optional

Read through the following instructions before you begin so you'll understand what kinds of threads, cords, yarns, and strings work best for the various parts of the tassel.

1 Begin by cutting a cardboard rectangle 3 in. to 4 in. wide and a little longer than you want your finished tassel to be. If the tassel is intended for a garment, you'll probably want to keep it between 2 in. and 3 in. and not too full. You don't want a fat, fluffy tassel that looks as if it should be hanging from a key on your armoire.

2 For a garment's tassel, choose threads and yarns that lie flat. Ordinary metallic and rayon sewing threads make lustrous tassels, and they blend beautifully with slightly heavier cords and fine yarns. Ribbon floss and 1/16-in. satin ribbons work well, too. There are no rules as to how many different threads you should use or how many times you should wrap them.

3 Hold the cut ends of the threads against one edge of the cardboard, then wrap them until they're as full as you want them. The wrapping doesn't need to be evenly done; this isn't a science. If you are using lightweight threads, take hold of the cut ends from two or three spools of thread along with a cord or two so that you can wrap them around the card at the same time.

ANATOMY OF A TASSEL

Hanging cord

Head

Neck

Skirt

The story of how I came to use tassels on my garments begins with something that happened a long time ago.

I was raised in a conservative Midwestern farm community where folks stayed close to home. Traveling was done with spouses or families, always by car, and a trip to the next state was a big deal. In the early 1950s, my mother went alone to a convention in New Orleans as the local representative of a traditional women's organization. I have a vivid memory of my father driving over dusty country back roads, hurrying to catch the train that would take Mom to this remote and outlandish place.

She'd donned a basic-black dress and a big black straw picture hat for her travels. She'd styled her hair over something that closely resembled a rat's nest into what she called a "chignon" and what most local folks simply called a "bun." Never mind, in my mind's eye the result was Loretta Young chic. Mom was the epitome of sophistication as she left on her daring adventure.

When she returned, she was full of stories, but the only one I remember was about her visit to Bourbon Street. (I'm convinced she started the evening with a mint julep, but she didn't tell that part.) She described a stripper's dance, complete with finger motions illustrating the talented dancer's ability to coordinate the swing of her tassels, first in one direction, then the other, then in opposition to each other.

My brothers and I looked at each other in disbelief, and Dad was laughing so hard he had to wipe tears from his eyes. As Mom told that story, I saw for the first time a human, worldly side of both parents that I hadn't seen before.

> *Then I remembered my mom's adventure in New Orleans and knew exactly how to solve my problem.*

My story fast-forwards to a sewing crisis 40 years later. I was attaching copper rivets, like the ones used on denim jeans, as the final embellishments on a vest that I was doing as a commission. I'd already pounded four of the pesky things on the front of the vest and was adding the last when my hammer slipped and put a hole through all the layers of my vest.

Mind you, my mantra has been, "There's no such thing as a mistake when you're doing fabric collage," but now I felt like adding "except this time" along with my expletives. To compound the disaster, the little hole I'd produced was located inconveniently at the bust point—just where I didn't want to draw attention.

In a desperate and unsuccessful attempt to think of a way to salvage the vest, my ideas eventually descended to the ridiculous. Feeling defeated, I told myself sarcastically, "I ought to just hang a tassel from that little hole and be done with it." Then I remembered my mom's adventure in New Orleans and knew exactly how to solve my problem.

I made a tiny buttonhole out of the slit I'd inadvertently made, then found a perfect little brass button shaped like a rose (my mother's name was also Rosemary). To the button I attached a lovely little tassel made in the subtle colors of the almost-ruined vest. The tassel drew the eye away from the point of destruction, it was removable for laundering, and it could be worn on either side of the reversible garment. I named that vest "Mama Goes to New Orleans" and sent it to its new home. (I hope its owner someday hears this story.)

4 When you've wrapped enough threads, snip them off so that the cut ends line up along the same edge of the cardboard that the first cut ends did.

5 To tie the wrapped threads into a bundle, cut a 5-in. length of a strong tassel thread or another strong cord that will blend in.

6 Slip that 5-in. thread under the tassel threads opposite its cut ends (see the top illustration at right). Use this cord to bundle the tassel thread and tie a tight knot around them.

7 Next, cut the tassel threads free of the cardboard at the edge opposite your knot (see the center illustration at right).

8 Make the cord that will be used for hanging into a loop as long as you want, then tie the two ends together in an overhand knot. For most garment tassels, 1 in. to 2 in. is long enough for the hanging cord, unless you want the tassel to have lots of swing.

9 Part your tassel threads where they're tied together (see the bottom illustration at right), then drape them over the knot of the hanging cord.

10 To wrap the tassel's neck, choose a strong, smooth cord or heavy thread. Dental floss will work like a needle threader to help you pull the loose working end of the wrapping cord through the back of the wrapped neck so that you will not have to tie a visible knot.

11 Fold the floss in half to form a loop. Firmly hold your tassel and the dental floss, loop end up, between the thumb and forefinger of one hand so that the cut ends of the floss trail down several inches past where the neck will end. Grasp the tassel and dental floss just below the hidden knot of the hanging cord (see the left illustration on p. 164).

MAKING A TASSEL

Bundling the Tassel Thread

Insert a 5-in. thread under the tassel threads to bundle them.

Tying and Snipping the Tassel

Attaching a Cord for Hanging

12 Next, slip one end of the wrapping cord under that same thumb so that this short end lies parallel to the dental floss and the tassel's skirt cords.

13 Use the wrapping cord's long end to begin the neck just below the hidden knot, wrapping it tightly from the top of the tassel toward the bottom. It should wrap over itself and the dental floss leaving the loop of floss exposed above the wrapping (see the center illustration on p. 164). As you wind, butt each coil exactly against the one before so that you get an even, neat neck.

You can vary the length of the wrapped neck to suit the size of the tassel, but for a garment I recommend making it no longer than ¼ in. to ½ in. When the neck is as long as you want it, retrace your wrapping from the bottom of the tassel back to the top. Again, make sure to wrap the

Using Dental Floss for a Neat Neck

Dental floss

Fold the dental floss in half to form a loop, then grasp the floss loop end up and the tassel just below the hidden neck of the hanging cord.

Wrapping the Neck

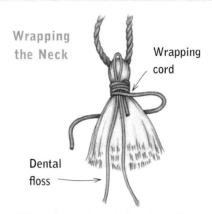

Wrapping cord

Dental floss

Wrap the cord just below the hidden neck and over the dental floss, but leave a loop of floss exposed above the wrapping.

The Clean Finish

Wrapping cord

Dental floss

Thread the wrapping cord through the dental-floss loop.

second layer of coils side-by-side as neatly as the first.

14 When you reach the top, thread the free end of the wrapping cord through the loop in the dental floss as shown in the illustration above right.

15 Clip the tail of the wrapping cord so that it is about 2 in. long, then pull on the two free ends of the dental floss. The loop in the dental floss will pull the wrapping cord's tail underneath the coils of wrapping and out through the bottom of the neck.

16 Finally, cut both ends of the wrapping cord flush with the bottom of the neck.

From here, you're on your own. You can embellish the neck with beads, charms, or stitching, and you can add charms to the skirt of the tassel. Even if you never learn another tassel technique, this basic one can keep you occupied for a lifetime designing tassels. They are a great "take-along" project, so gather up your almost-used-up spools of thread and special yarns, head for the soccer game, and start tasseling!

Applying Shisha Mirrors and Flat Disks by Machine

I've been fascinated by shisha mirrors since my uncle sent me a little pair of shisha-adorned shoes and a shisha-embellished vest from Pakistan when he was building roads there in the 1950s. Every time I use shisha on one of my garments, I find myself wondering what life had been like for the children who wore such elegant little garments in Pakistan, India, and Afghanistan.

Shisha mirrors seem to be harder to come by in recent years (see Resources on p. 168). My favorites are the antique grayish shisha mirrors and the rainbow, peacock-colored shisha that are plain colored on one side and have a colored mirror on the other. Because they are handmade, they often have bubbles and other irregularities in the glass.

These shisha are lightweight and washable, but their edges are rough and uneven. Their jagged edges would saw right through their thread trappings if they tumbled in a washing machine, so I only wash them by hand. I usually add them to a collaged garment after the final laundering, just to be safe.

Another type called perfect shishas are machine made and look like regular mirrors. They are much heavier, and because of their mirrored backs they must be dry-cleaned. I'd only use them on fabric artwork that's to hang on a wall.

Shisha can be applied in the traditional way by hand, but I'm always looking for a way to transform hand-stitching methods to machine methods. I've combined several techniques to come up with my way of applying them.

To try out my methods, you'll need the following materials:

- Shisha mirrors or other flat disks such as coins, Mylar shapes, and acrylic mirrors
- Water-soluble stabilizer
- Spray starch or a fine-mist spray water bottle
- An embroidery hoop that will fit under your machine's presser foot, optional
- A 12-in. square of tulle (fine netting)
- A fine-tipped marking pen
- A sewing machine set up for free-motion stitching (see p. 40)
- An iron
- A Teflon press cloth

PREPARING THE STABILIZER

My method of applying shisha involves using free-motion embroidery on a stabilizer to make a medallion-shaped frame that's larger than your shisha. That frame will then be sewn on top of your artwork to hold the disk in place. Below are three different ways in which you can prepare your stabilizer to be stitched upon.

Variation 1 In this first method, the stitching surface consists of multiple layers of bonded water-soluble stabilizer. You can do this method without a hoop.

1 Cut four layers of lightweight water-soluble stabilizer or two layers of extra-heavy stabilizer into 6-in. squares.

2 To bond the stabilizer, spread out all the layers on an ironing board. Check your starch can or spray bottle to make sure it sprays a fine mist without spitting large drops of liquid. Hold the spray 18 in. above the stabilizer, then move it quickly as you spray the air above so that only tiny moisture particles land on the stabilizer. It's important that this misting be very light because the moisture will make a tiny hole everywhere it lands.

3 Next, quickly stack the squares of stabilizer on one end of the Teflon press sheet, and fold the other end over to cover the stack.

4 Press with a moderate iron to bond the layers into one.

Variation 2 The second method uses bonded multiple layers of stabilizer with tulle. Again, you do not need to use a hoop. Follow the steps for variation 1, but this time sandwich a layer of tulle between just two layers of either lightweight or heavy stabilizer before you bond them.

Variation 3 In this third method, the stitching surface consists of multiple layers of lightweight water-soluble stabilizer, and you use a hoop. Make sure your embroidery hoop is thin enough to slip under the presser foot on your machine.

1 Cut four pieces of regular water-soluble stabilizer or two pieces of heavy stabilizer 3 in. larger than the diameter of your hoop.

2 Lay them in a stack over the larger ring of the hoop, and fit the smaller hoop inside so that the stabilizer is held tautly. When you place the hoop with the stabi-

Shisha
outline

Stitch three times along the stitching line.

lizer under your presser foot, be sure that the stabilizer is against the work surface.

MAKING A THREAD FRAME

When you've decided which method you're going to use to stabilize your shisha's thread frames, the sewing fun begins.

1 Once you have prepared a stitching surface, use a fine-tipped marking pen to trace around the disk on the stabilizer, then lay the disk aside for now. If you are using a mirror or disk that's ½ in. across or smaller, draw a second circle ⅛ in. inside of the first. If your disk is larger than ½ in., draw the second circle a little less than ¼ in. inside of the first. The stitching that holds a larger disk in place will stretch out of shape and allow the disk to fall out if the central hole in the medallion is too large.

2 To set up your machine, attach a darning foot or other presser foot for free-motion sewing, adjust the machine for a straight stitch, and use regular thread in the bobbin and needle.

3 Insert the needle somewhere on the inner circle line, and bring the bobbin thread to the top of your work.

4 Holding both thread tails securely, stitch three times around this circle (see the illustration above left). Stop with your needle down, and snip the thread tails.

5 Continuing to use free-motion stitching, follow one of the stitching patterns

shown in the illustration above right. Be sure the radiating stitches cross the triple-stitched center circle each time you come to it, otherwise your stitching will fall apart as soon as you wash away the stabilizer. This is especially crucial if you aren't using tulle with the stabilizer.

6 Once you have stitched around the entire medallion, anchor the radiating lines with a spiral of stitches (see the top illustration on the facing page). If you're using a stabilizer-plus-tulle sandwich, you can remove your medallion from the sewing machine, carefully cut out the unstitched center, and then slip it back under the needle for further stitching. If you haven't used tulle, leave the center intact.

7 Lower your needle again into the inner circle line, then overlay that inner circle of stitches with narrow satin stitches to neaten and strengthen the frame. I find it's easiest to do free-motion satin stitching, but it can also be done with normal feed-dogs-up stitching.

You can make these satin stitches look a lot like handmade chain stitches by using a technique that Virgie Fisher, an artwear teacher and artist, showed me.

1 Start by attaching a presser foot designed for satin stitching to your machine, and make sure the feed dogs are dropped.

2 Set your machine for a 6mm-wide zigzag stitch.

3 Next, arrange the medallion under your needle so that the satin stitch will lie on top of and be parallel to the stitching on the inner circle that you stitched around three times.

4 Stitch eight zigzag stitches in place, raise your presser foot, and move it one-half stitch to the right. Making sure the needle is ready for the left stitch of the next zigzag, lower it by hand into the middle of the first set of zigzag stitches.

5 Now do a second set of eight in-place zigzag stitches. Continue to use this technique to overlap sets of stitches around the entire inner circle (see the illustration below). It takes time, but it gives a fantastic finished look to your medallion.

6 Make as many medallions as you expect to use. If you're using an embroidery hoop, you can probably do several of them, depending on their size, before removing the hoop.

7 Next, carefully remove the excess stabilizer (and tulle, if you've used it) from around the medallions. Rinse the medallions in tepid water to remove the stabilizer, then blot out the excess moisture, and allow them to air-dry. If you're impatient to use them, as I usually am, you can use a warm iron to press them between layers of paper towels until they're dry.

8 Using a UHU or another washable glue stick, secure your shisha or disk where you want it on your collage. If it looks as if the medallion's central hole is so large that the shisha might fall out, use waterproof fabric glue. Otherwise, only a light glue is needed to hold the shisha in place until the thread medallion can take over. Pin or glue the medallion in place, too.

9 When the glue is dry and the medallion is secured, remove the presser foot from your machine so you can stitch close to the shisha's edge. I always warn students

ANCHORING THE RADIATING LINES WITH SPIRALS

to be extremely careful because if your needle strikes the disk, the needle and the mirror are likely to shatter.

10 To hold the medallion in place, free-motion stitch once around the edge of the mirror.

11 Put the darning foot back on the machine.

12 Continue to stitch in a spiral around the medallion to secure it. Be sure to stitch out to the very ends of the radiating lines of stitching, or they'll poke up when your garment is laundered.

As you've probably figured out, this technique isn't just for round shapes. You can create original patterns for frames in any shape—rectangular, oval, or free-form. Even flat rocks or gemstones can be held in place with these thread medallions.

MACHINE-SEWING CHAIN STITCHES THAT LOOK HAND-SEWN

Stitch eight zigzag stitches in place, move the presser foot one-half stitch to the right, and sew a second set of in-place stitches. Continue in this manner around the circle.

Resources

Sewing Supplies

THE BUTTON SHOPPE
4744 Oakfield Circle
Carmichael, CA 95608
(916) 488-5350
www.TheButtonShoppe.net
Large selection of buttons. Catalog.

CLOTILDE INC.
2 Sew Smart Way B8031
Stevens Point, WI 54481-8031
(800) 772-2891
Threads and notions. Catalog.

COUNTERPOINT BUTTONS
Jean Keeshin
321 South Main St., PMB#40
Sebastopol, CA 95472
(707) 829-3529
Art buttons. Catalog.

DHARMA TRADING CO.
Box 150916
San Rafael, CA 94915
(800) 542-5227
www.dharmatrading.com
Fabric paints and dyes. Catalog.

DISCOUNT BEAD HOUSE
P. O. Box 186
The Plains, OH 45780-0186
(800) 423-2319
e-mail: polymer@frognet.net
Silamide thread and beads. Catalog.

JONESTONES
33865 United Ave.
Pueblo, CO 81001
(800) 216-0616
www.jonestones.com
Foil for surface design.

KREINIK
3106 Timanus Ln., Suite #101
Baltimore, MD 21244
(800) 354-4255
Novelty threads.

MADIERA USA
P. O. Box 6068
Laconia, NH 03247-6068
(800) 225-3001
Novelty threads.

NANCY'S NOTIONS
P. O. Box 583
Beaver Dam, WI 53916-0683
(800) 833-0690
www.nancysnotions.com
Threads and notions. Catalog.

SEWJOURNER PATTERNS
Rosemary Eichorn
166 Timber View Rd.
Soquel, CA 95073
sewjourn@mixedsig.com
Vest and tunic patterns.

TREADLEARTS
25834 Narbonne Ave.
Lomita, CA 90717
(888) 322-4745
Shisha mirrors.

SULKY OF AMERICA
3113 Broadpoint Dr.
Harbor Heights, FL 33983
(800) 874-4115
www.sulky.com
Threads and stabilizers.

YLI CORPORATION
161 West Main St.
Rock Hill, SC 29730
(800) 296-8139
e-mail: ylicorp@rhtc.net
Novelty threads.

Books

Itten, Johannes. *The Art of Color.* New York: Van Nostrand Reinhold, 1973.
Originally published in Germany under the title Kunst der Farbe, *this book discusses progressive color theory.*

Dunnewold, Jane. *Complex Cloth.* Bothell, Wash.: Fiber Studio Press, 1996.
This book describes surface design techniques.

Lauer, David A. *Design Basics.* Fort Worth, Tex.: Harcourt Brace Jovanovich College Publishers, 1990.

Wessel, Dianna Swim. *Inspiration Odyssey.* Bothell, Wash.: Fiber Studio Press, 1996.
Refer to this book for its chapter on bindings.

Nadelstern, Paula. *Kaleidoscopes & Quilts.* Lafayette, Calif.: C&T Publishing, 1996.

Ericson, Lois. *Opening and Closing.* Salem, Ore.: Eric's Press, 1996.
This book discusses various garment closures.

Welch, Nancy. *Tassels: The Fanciful Embellishment.* Asheville, N.C.: Lark Books, 1992.

Index

Note: references in italic indicate a visual reference.